WEALTHY WAYS

Journey to true financial triumph
and staying successful

TAYO AROWOJOLU

Wealthy Ways: Journey to True Financial Triumph and Staying Successful - Tayo Arowojolu

Unless otherwise stated, all scripture quotations are taken from the Holy Bible, New King James Version (NKJV). Other versions cited are NIV, KJV, GNB, God's Word, MSG, LEB, and NLT.

ISBN 978-1-907734-15-1
First Edition, First Printing October 2016

No part of this publication may be produced, distorted or transmitted in any form or by any means, including photocopying, recording or other electronic or mechanical methods, without the prior written permission of the publisher, or except in the case of brief quotations embodied in critical reviews and certain other noncommercial uses permitted by copyright law.

For permission requests, write to the publisher, addressed "Attention: Permission Coordinator" at the email address below:

Covenant Publishing
samadewunmi@btinternet.com

Covenant Publishing is part of New Covenant Church
Charity Registered in England & Wales number 1004343
Registered Address: 506-510 Old Kent Road. LONDON SE1 5BA

Copyright © November 2016, Tayo Arowojolu
All rights reserved

Cover Design by Covenant Publishing Team
Published by Covenant Publishing
Printed in the United Kingdom

TABLE OF CONTENT

Dedication	v
Acknowledgement	vii
Foreword	ix
Preface	11
Introduction: Setting the Scene	13
Chapter 1: Spiritual Building Blocks	23
Chapter 2: Character Building	49
Chapter 3: Capacity Building - Purpose	73
Chapter 4: Capacity Building – Skills Development	89
Chapter 5: Breaking the Yoke of Poverty	113
Chapter 6: Access to Financial Triumph through His Covenant	129
Chapter 7: Access to Spiritual Speed	147
Chapter 8: How to Make and Sustain Wealth by Appreciation	167
Chapter 9: Life Learning Building Block – The Practical Art of Making and Keeping Money	183
Chapter 10: Prayers	199
66 Scriptural Nuggets to Financial Breakthrough	205
Your Personal Action Sheet	239

Dedication

This book is dedicated to my life coach and discipler, late Revd. Timothy Kolade, and to my children Nifemi, Damini, Damisi and Pemiwa.

Acknowledgement

'Tayo, God wants your life' That was a reverberating statement I got from the pulpit from my discipler and life coach late Revd. Timothy Kolade, Deputy General Overseer, New Covenant Church. That word re-energised and lifted me out of what could have been a frustrating experience. Hence, I will forever, thank him for speaking to my life and being there always. He is alive in Christ, and his legacy lives forever in our hearts. I am dedicating this book to his legacy.

Further, I want to appreciate the apostolic anointing on my spiritual father, Revd. Dr. Paul Jinadu, for being unique in my life, and never getting tired of being a father. There are indeed many teachers, but you are our father indeed and in need.

I also want to appreciate and acknowledge a man of God that I have never met, but I have listened to his messages on wealth, Bishop David Abioye of Winners Chapel. Listening to your messages whenever I had my 'silent therapies' opened my understanding to some aspects of wealth creating teachings. Some of them, I have repeated in this book.

I cannot but thank the following members of New Covenant Church who helped in editing this book. Akinola Morenike, Ijomanta Maureen, Morin Duntoye, Bola Adebajo and Wande Showunmi. I also want to mention the following, who partner with me on a monthly basis of which seed I have invested in this book. You would not like me to name names, but please forgive me: the Arises, the Kuniyis, Femi Loye, Adebajos, Abimbolas, Seun Osho, Onikans, Pastor and Mrs Victor Olatunji, Taiwos, Showunmis, and Idowus. Your reward is special in the harvest. I also want to thank all the members of the New Covenant Church Edmonton, and all the branches within the Edmonton Conference.

And as always my publisher Rev Sam O. Adewunmi, who must be mentioned and encouraged to keep on keeping up.

My charming wife Bimbo aka 'Mama' a rock of Gibraltar, and on whose broad shoulders I rested during the challenging times, I pray God will perfect your wisdom. Nifemi, Damisi, Damini and Pemiwa, you have brought me exceeding joy this year, and I also dedicate this book to you as signs of a bright future. God will preserve you for Himself. Amen.

Above all, a great appreciation to God. Who can fathom your immense love for us? No one. Thank you for being changeless.

Foreword

> "Like everything in life, it is not what happens to you, but how you respond to it that counts."

> "There are three types of people in this world. Firstly, there are people who make things happen. Then there are people who watch things happen. Lastly, there are people who ask, what happened? Which do you want to be?"
> *Steve Backley, The Champion in all of Us: 12 Rules for Success*

It is not every time that one finds the privilege to witness a set of circumstances that would change one's focus and one's life. If you encounter such in a lifetime, rejoice, again I say rejoice. God has blessed me and has catapulted me to an enviable position. I guess we all can say that, however, He has a way of using tests, challenges and living testimonies to change the course of our life.

This book speaks to such testimony. My understanding of wealth and making money would not have been complete or ripe if I did not experience a life-changing experience in March 2009. I realised that the line between being healthy and being dead, being wealthy and being poor is so thin. How could I explain standing up, attending a church service in a moment and then finding later in the day my body could not do that which I demanded of it? Within a twinkle of a moment, I found myself in the hospital, and minutes after on the way being wheeled to the theatre for an operation, and another one within a year! It was going to be the end of my full-time work as a solicitor.

The whole story and how I gained my life and my wealth back, is a story I have told over and over again. It is not what I can fully share in this piece. However, the lessons I learnt, and the truth of how wealth can be perpetuated in a Christian's life are the foundational principles of this book. Having made all, lost all and then gained much more, a Job's tale takes the grace of God and an immense understanding of how He sustains His children in wealth for His purpose. All the dynamics, and the changing narratives of modern day acquisition of wealth and the need to eschew materialistic tendency are captured between the pages of this book. It took me seven years to write, as I got overwhelmed and distracted many times as I re-lived some of the experiences.

I am sure, you will benefit from reading the book, and affirm to live your life based on God's standard and not man's formula.

Enjoy.

Preface

This book is based on a series of teachings God laid on my heart regarding awakening His children to the promise of financial triumph. Through these series of teachings, I covered the essence and principles of how financial triumph can be achieved at any point in one's Christian life. This book covers the core of these teachings under the following four areas:

1. Spiritual building;
2. Character building;
3. Capacity building (and Purpose); and
4. Life learning.

We will also look at how to break the curse of poverty and how to operate under obedience, God's covenants and how to leverage your journey towards financial triumph.

At the end of this book, the reader will have an action plan which will be derived from his personal reflection based on his learning, in addition to a confession and meditation chapter titled "66 scriptural nuggets to financial breakthrough". These nuggets provide the reader with a daily tool for confession and meditation, to ensure an enduring and impactful translation of the knowledge gained from reading, into practical daily living.

I have an assurance that reading and practicing the knowledge that comes from this book will take you to a position of financial triumph in Jesus' name. Amen!

Happy reading and blessings!

Tayo Arowojolu

Introduction

Setting the Scene

Indeed, there is a season of financial triumph that can be experienced by everyone. This is God's promise to us, and it is real.

God's kingdom is built upon principles, laws, and promises and when we activate them, walk and work in them, God fulfils His promises and gives us exactly that which He has promised.

In this book, we will go through the journey of how to obtain our financial breakthrough and triumph by studying how to combine four building blocks which I term biblical touchstones for financial triumph:

1. Spiritual building blocks;
2. Character building blocks;
3. Capacity building blocks; and
4. Life learning building blocks

Before considering each block, our first point of call is to understand what 'triumph' means. In understanding the meaning of triumph, we can then begin to visualise and create a picture of what exactly financial triumph looks like and why it is essential.

The Dictionary defines 'triumph' as:

- Being victorious or successful; to win.
- Being able to rejoice over a success or victory; to exult.
- To receive honour upon return from a victory or conquest.
- A noteworthy or spectacular success.
- Exultation or rejoicing over victory or success.
- A public celebration in ancient Rome to welcome a returning victorious commander and his army.
- A public celebration or spectacular pageant.

Triumph means victory, and to have victory, there is a natural connotation that there must have been battles which were fought and which resulted in overcoming and victorious experiences. In Deuteronomy 1:6-8, God stirred the hearts of the children of Israel to this reality:

"The Lord our God spoke to us in Horeb, saying: 'You have dwelt long enough at this mountain. Turn

Introduction: Setting the Scene

and take your journey, and go to the mountains of the Amorites, to all the neighbouring places in the plain, in the mountains and in the lowland, in the South and on the seacoast, to the land of the Canaanites and to Lebanon, as far as the great river, the River Euphrates. See, I have set the land before you; go in and possess the land which the Lord swore to your fathers – to Abraham, Isaac, and Jacob – to give to them and their descendants after them."

Also, see Deuteronomy 2:2-3:

"And the Lord spoke to me, saying: 'You have skirted this mountain long enough; turn northward."

These verses imply that God challenged their complacency that nothing was going to happen regarding the next level of victory if all they were prepared to do was to sit, watch and wait.

Against this background of the definition of triumph is how God wants us to activate His Word.

In 3 John 1:2, the wish of God for us about financial triumph was declared. A paraphrased version of this verse is,

"My wish above every other thing for you is that you prosper and be in health, even as your soul prospers."

This, in its simplicity, confirms God's intent is to ensure you as a child of His, enjoy financial victory.

That scripture is like a two sided coin because it also encapsulates the entire desire of everyone. We all want to prosper in every area of our lives; we want to live well and live long. We also do not want to lose our soul.

So, it is God's will for us, and we desire it for ourselves. The question we then need to ask ourselves is if it is God's intent for us to arrive at a place of financial triumph, and we desire this for ourselves; how come most of the time we find ourselves not arriving or not consistently operating in the place of financial triumphs?

Also, keep in mind that we know according to Numbers 23:19, God cannot lie:

> *"God is not a man, that He should lie, nor a son of man, that He should repent. Has He said, and will He not do?"*

The Bible takes the time to describe this paradox. Romans 8:19 states:

> *"For the earnest expectation of the creation eagerly waits for the revealing of the sons of God."*

This, in essence, tells us that creation itself waits, fervently with much keenness and in anticipation of the manifestation of the sons of God which is yet to come. We are causing the delay; God has done His part.

Solomon in Ecclesiastes 10:6-7 also provides a graphic description to this mishap and contradiction of the life of an unfulfilled man or woman. He says,

Introduction: Setting the Scene

"Folly is set in many exalted places while rich men sit in humble places. I have seen slaves riding on horses and princes walking like slaves on the land".

We, therefore, can come to a reasonable and objective conclusion that even the word is clear on the fact that this manifestation and promise of financial triumph may not take place fully in the life of the deserving. See also, Galatians 4: 1-3:

"Now I say that the heir, as long as he is a child, does not differ at all from a slave, though he is master of all, but is under guardians and stewards until the time appointed by the father. Even so we, when we were children, were in bondage under the elements of the world."

In our day to day life, we can clearly see this mishap through what has been referred to as three distinct categories of people in work:

1. Common Workers
2. Managers and
3. Leaders

1. COMMON WORKERS

This group consists of people that work 9am-5pm. They work for other people as employees and very often lack the commitment for the real job. This group tends to spend time checking their clock at work. As for them, there is a cut-off point after which work can no longer be done. This category of workers is unlikely to experience the kind of exponential financial breakthrough that is envisaged in this book. Such readers should use this book to cause a sea change in their life.

The idea is not to abandon your job, if you are in this category, the aim is to encourage you to set your expectations higher and focus on being a leader.

2. MANAGERS

This group of workers is slightly an advanced group than the common workers. Within their roles or as a result of their professions, opportunity becomes available to them to engage in overtime; however, without the overtime, they cannot pay their bills, can't pay their mortgage, and as such, they have not arrived at a place of financial robustness. This group of people give so much of their time to work that it is very often tiresome for them to engage in the things of God or to give proper service time to God. This group needs to step up to occupy their positions and focus on becoming a leader. In the Bible, Jacob started out in the first category. He worked for Laban and became a manager at some point after almost years of labour. A time came when he went to Laban and said to him,

> *"Give me my wives and my children for whom I have served you, and let me go; for you know my service which I have done for you"* (Genesis 30:26).

Introduction: Setting the Scene

To move from category 1 or 2 to the 3rd category, which we will consider shortly, is not an easy feat. It takes conviction based on will power. At times, it could be God himself dragging you from that position, or using a man of God to give you direction. It could also be like in Jacob's situation, the amount of enslavement or abuse in a particular position, which would galvanise you to move in any event. In my case, God used my General Overseer to speak the word of God to me and cause a remarkable change in my life.

3. LEADERS

The next group of workers are the leaders. Leaders are workers who lead in their art and trade. These people are owners of their businesses and their trades. A leader does not check his time to know when it is time to go home just as a casual worker does. He knows the business belongs to him and that he must deliver. When things are going well with the business, he enjoys, and when things do go wrong, he finds a way to deliver. As a leader, you are exposed to love and hatred. A leader must look up to God always and learn to be a total leader. A leader must not be in the same category as a common worker.

The ultimate plan for us is to stand as leaders as this is the place of entry into financial triumph. My aim at the end of this book, is to bring you to a point, where mentally, spiritually and physically you become a leader;

that is the place where financial prosperity and triumph begin. This is God's desire for you: Psalm 35:27 says

> "Let them shout for joy and be glad, who favour my righteous cause; and let them say continually, let the Lord be magnified, Who has pleasure in the prosperity of His servant."

Jesus knew what He would do (John 6:6). He knows what He would do concerning us. His plan is to prosper us:

> "For I know the plans I have for you," declares the Lord, "plans to prosper you and not to harm you, plans to give you hope and a future" (Jeremiah 29:11).

If His desire is to prosper you and grant you financial triumph, you need to ask yourself:

- What exactly is stopping me from entering into my financial triumph?
- Do I wish to come into my season of financial freedom?
- Is my situation too hopeless to experience this triumph?
- Is this just a cliché which cannot be achieved?
- What do I need to do regarding my character, my spiritual life, and my physical life to get there?

Introduction: Setting the Scene

Working through the four pillars and blocks, this book will support you to find answers to these questions. Let us remind ourselves of what these are:

1. Spiritual building blocks;
2. Character building blocks;
3. Capacity building blocks; and
4. Life learning building blocks.

WEALTHY WAYS

Chapter 1

Spiritual Building Blocks

A certain story in the Bible will help us understand the essence of the spiritual building. We will begin this teaching from that point.

In 2 King 4: 1-7, there was a widow, whose husband was a man of God. He had died, and she was in a real financial mess!

The story goes;

> "One day the wife of a man from the guild of prophets called out to Elisha, "Your servant my husband is dead. You well know what a good man he was, devoted to God. And now the man to whom he was in debt is on his way to collect by taking my two children as slaves." Elisha said, "I wonder how I can be of help. Tell me, what do you have in your house?" "Nothing," she said. "Well, I do have a little oil. "Here's what you do," said Elisha. "Go up and down the street and borrow jugs and bowls from all your neighbours. And not just a few – all you can get. Then come home and lock the door behind you, you and your sons. Pour oil into each container; when each is

full, set it aside." She did what he said. *She locked the door behind her and her sons; as they brought the containers to her, she filled them. When all the jugs and bowls were full, she said to one of her sons, "Another jug, please."* He said, *"That's it. There are no more jugs."* Then the oil stopped. *She went and told the story to the man of God. He said, "Go sell the oil and make good on your debts. Live, both you and your sons, on what's left."*

This story has a euphoric ending. It demonstrates the simple fact that no situation can be beyond God's redemptive power. There is no financial dilemma or challenge which His power cannot resolve. There are lessons to be learned from this story, and certainly, principles to follow:

There are five key principles from this story. These principles serve as the bedrock in learning how to lay a strong spiritual foundation for a secure financial triumph.

PRINCIPLE 1

YOU MUST KNOW THAT YOU ARE QUALIFIED

Firstly, you must know that you can achieve a financial breakthrough. We know this because the text denotes that this situation happened to a "certain woman." A certain woman in this text means anyone. It means it can be relevant to you or any individual who chooses to tap into the power and lessons in this story. This woman (representing anyone), was in a terrible place financially.

Chapter 1: Spiritual Building Blocks

Note and understand that you are a beneficiary of financial triumph legacy regardless of the situation you find yourself, because of the simple fact that you are a child of God. Let's consider some passages that bring this reality to life for us.

2 Corinthians 8:9

> *"For you know the grace of our Lord Jesus Christ, that though He was rich, yet for your sakes He became poor, that you, through His poverty might become rich."*

Jeremiah 17:7-8

> *"Blessed is the man who trusts in the Lord, and whose hope is the Lord. For he shall be like a tree planted by the waters, which spreads out its roots by the river, and will not fear when heat comes, but its leaf will be green, and will not be anxious in the year of drought, nor will cease from yielding fruit."*

These passages show what we are qualified for (Jeremiah 17: 7-8) and why we are qualified for it (2 Corinthians 8:9) – God's willingness to exchange His riches for our poverty. You are no longer poor; you are rich. God had by sacrificing His son, given us a legacy of prosperity. Jesus became poor so that we can be rich. A pictorial snapshot of what this looks like can be gazed into through the lens of Jeremiah 17:7-8.

There had been a previous process that now allows you to enjoy wealth. He (Christ) took away any curse of poverty on the cross. Perhaps, you or your family (generation) had been placed under a curse of poverty; the Bible tells us that such a curse has been lifted.

> *"Christ has redeemed us from the curse of the law, having become a curse for us, for it is written, "Cursed is everyone who hangs on a tree that the blessing of Abraham might come..." Gal 3:13-14.*

Interesting? Yes, you are a seed of Abraham by your connection to Christ through salvation. Hence, Abraham's blessings are yours.

Taking it further, we can ask ourselves: What are the blessings of Abraham? These blessings are in several passages of the Bible, but let me limit them to the one that started it all: Genesis 12:1-3

> *"Now the Lord had said to Abram: Get out of your country, from your family and from your father's house, to a land that I will show you. I will make you a great nation; I will bless you and make your name great; and you shall be a blessing. I will bless those who bless you, and I will curse him who curses you; and in you all the families of the earth shall be blessed."*

Such wonderful blessings and heritage, we have; and if you take the time to study the life of Abraham, we see that he was blessed throughout his lifetime. Gen 24:1 says,

> *"Now Abraham was old, well advanced in age; and the Lord had blessed Abraham in all things."*

Galatians 3:29 says,

> "*And if you are Christ's then you are Abraham's seed and heirs according to the promise*"

That is precisely how God has, and shall bless you. Amen.

This woman in our story knew who she was. She knew which connection the husband had, hence her words "*Your servant my husband is dead, and you know that he revered the Lord.*"

So, the first question you need to ask yourself in your journey to true financial triumph is "do you know who you are in Christ?"

PRINCIPLE 2

YOU MUST CHECK WHERE YOU ARE

The second principle in your journey towards financial triumph is that of a self-assessment. Know that a "self-assessment" of one's self is always vital. This confident woman did. This lady knew her situation; she recognised that she was in a bad financial state. She had made a self-assessment of herself and had a clear insight into what the implications of these were. She knew her children and herself were in a financial hole.

Take a self-assessment of yourself, be true to yourself and understand where exactly you are, regarding that assessment. There is an adage which says that when you are in a hole, you stop digging. You must know your position in life, know the state of your finances and know whether you need a financial breakthrough.

See 1 Chronicles 4:9; it is what is commonly referred to as the prayer of Jabez. We read how Jabez prayed that most essential and desperate prayer. He knew and must have heard several versions of the story of his birth. He knew how his mother rejected him and gave him a bad name. He was aware of the storyline of his lineage. He cried out against the background of his name for a change from God.

1 Chronicles 4:9

> *"Now Jabez was more honourable than his brothers, and his mother called his name Jabez, saying, "Because I bore him in pain." And Jabez called on the God of Israel saying, "Oh that You would bless me indeed, and enlarge my territory, that your hand would be with me, and that You would keep me from evil, that I may not cause pain!" So God granted him what he requested!"*

Jabez's prayers were answered because he knew where he was. No General set out to battle without appraising his position. He was aware that his situation was bad. He must have carried out a self-assessment.

Chapter 1: Spiritual Building Blocks

Another example in the process of self-assessment is the children of Israel. They were to be in Egypt for 400 years. God had said the following to Abraham,

> "*Then He said to Abram: "Know certainly that your descendants will be strangers in a land that is not theirs, and will serve them, and they will afflict them four hundred years." Genesis 15:13.*

However, they stayed for 430 years. However, the day they realised that they had stayed beyond the time, and had started to suffer too much humiliation from slavery, they took a self-assessment of their situation and cried out. Moreover, as we see from Exodus 3:7-8, God answered them:

> *And the Lord said: "I have surely seen the oppression of My people who are in Egypt, and have heard their cry because of their taskmasters, for I know their sorrows. So I have come down to deliver them out of the hand of the Egyptians, and to bring them up from that land to a good and large land, to a land flowing with milk and honey, to the place of the Canaanites and the Hittites and the Amorites and the Perizzites and the Hivites and the Jebusites."*

Even the prodigal son recognised that he was not born for suffering nor to eat the pods of pigs. He came to himself and said he needed to go back to his father. He would rather be a servant in his father's palace than be a pain in the pig shed. He conducted a self-assessment:

> *"But when he came to himself, he said, 'How many of my father's hired servants have bread enough and to spare, and I perish with hunger! 18 I will arise and go to my father and will say to him, "Father, I have sinned against heaven and before you, and I am no longer worthy to be called your son. Make me like one of your hired servants" (Luke 15:17-18).*

The woman in our story considered where she was financially. She did not find her position palatable.

She did not waste time; she cried out to the prophet. She was saved.

So, the second question you need to ask yourself in your journey to true financial triumph is "Do I know where I am financially? Have I carried out a self-assessment?" This is very instructive. Many people love to sing and quote the verse that 'Abraham's blessings are mine.' However, the question is, can you do what Abraham did? This passage of the Bible helps put it in perspective:

> *"Listen to Me, you who follow after righteousness, you who seek the Lord: Look to the rock from which you were hewn, and to the hole of the pit from which you were dug. Look to Abraham your father, and to Sarah who bore you; for I called him alone, and blessed him and increased him." For the Lord will comfort Zion, He will comfort all her waste places; He will make her wilderness like Eden, and her desert like the garden of the Lord; joy and gladness will be found in it, thanksgiving and the voice of melody" (Isaiah 51:1-3).*

Chapter 1: Spiritual Building Blocks

Verse 2. Look to Abraham your father 'for I called him and increased him'... Abraham paid his tithes, gave, he was faithful, blameless, and he loved, worshipped God and trusted God. Are you doing the same? Please read chapters 12 to 24 of Genesis for Abraham's various works.

Another passage that helps is found in John 8:39:

"They answered and said to Him, Abraham is our father. Jesus said to them, if you were Abraham's children, you would do the works of Abraham."

This passage is mind blowing. You can claim and emphasise your relationship with Abraham, but you will not partake or obtain any benefits with regards to that relationship, without doing what Abraham did.

PRINCIPLE 3

YOU MUST KNOW WHO CAN HELP YOU

The third principle is for us to cry out to a higher authority by faith.

Jabez did not cry or call out to man, or to the bank manager or the warriors in the city; he faced his God and cried unto Him. God answered him because he knew whom to call for help, and he knew his situation was bad.

The widow in 2 Kings 4 cried to a higher authority – her helper was not on the same level as she was, see Psalm 121: 1- 2 which says:

> *"I will lift up my eyes to the hills – from whence comes my help? My help comes from the Lord, Who made heaven and earth."*

Psalm 61:2 also says,

> *"When my heart is overwhelmed, lead me to the rock that is higher than I."*

Also, see Hebrews 7:7,

> *"And without doubt the lesser is blessed by the greater."*

This woman in our main story operated based on these verses - she went to a source that had more insight into spiritual things than she had.

In practical terms, it is relevant not just to approach the throne of grace in a crisis, but it is equally relevant that we have total belief that we can find help from that source.

> *"But without faith it is impossible to please Him, for he who comes to God must believe that He is, and that He is a rewarder of those who diligently seek Him" (Hebrews 11:6).*

God is superior to any other being. She cried out to God by seeking help from her prophet. In our desperation, we can go directly to God. He will direct us to whom to approach or not to approach. The woman's action does not denote that we should always approach men of God; it denotes that she had the discernment to

Chapter 1: Spiritual Building Blocks

approach a higher authority who could rely on godly wisdom to help her.

My experience has shown that we tend to seek help usually from those that cannot help themselves. Some so called helpers are too weak to help you in any way. Some of them are even scared of your challenges that going to them can cause you to lose faith.

God will not step down to help you; He will have to use someone. It is for you to sit down and carefully seek God's face and ask: who are the divine helpers that can help me in this situation? In your church, it may be your pastor, your prayer partner, an elder, a minister or even a friend in the church. At work, it could be your employer, your colleague, your line manager. In the house, it could be your spouse or your children. God can use anybody. Some people do not want to approach their spouse! Who else would help you in that situation? The key is, who is the Lord sending your way at the time of distress as a divine helper?

I recall some years ago when I had some challenges I could not deal with; I approached my discipler. He shared the weight with me, gave me some counselling, useful scriptures, and some ministry secrets. I followed his counsel. I became free from the bondage.

We know from the Bible and from personal experiences that God places divine helpers and gatekeepers our way. They are always there; the problem is discerning who they are and where they are. I will cite one unique biblical experience:

JOSEPH

Joseph was a unique person. From his childhood, he had always had someone in his life that favoured him. His father loved him so much more than his siblings that he made him a robe of many colours (Genesis 37:3-4). His brothers envied him so much that they sold him out to slave merchants (Genesis 37:26-28). The slave merchants took him to Egypt and sold him to the house of Potiphar, an officer, and captain of the guard (Genesis 37:36). We know that even as a slave in Potiphar's house, the Lord granted him favour there (Genesis 39:2-6). Later on, Potiphar's wife lied against him, got him in trouble, and he was consequently imprisoned (Genesis 39:20). However, even in prison, he was favoured by the prison governor (Genesis 39:21-23). While in prison, he met the baker and the butler to the Pharaoh of the time. As it happened, these two had dreams which Joseph correctly interpreted, that is, that the baker would be beheaded, while the butler would be restored to his post in the palace. He made a poignant request of the butler in Genesis 40:14, *'"but remember me when it is well with you, and please show kindness to me; make mention of me to Pharaoh and get me out of this house."*[1]

Chapter 1: Spiritual Building Blocks

Even though it was two years later and after Pharaoh had a dream, the butler remembered Joseph and advised Pharaoh that he could help him understand what his dream meant (Genesis 41:9-13). Joseph was sent for and called out of prison; he interpreted the dream and proffered solution. He was promoted and became the Prime Minister (Genesis 41:37-45). In a period of 13 years, Joseph's life had witnessed remarkable ups and downs, but he had come into a prominent position because of the divine interplay of destiny helpers (his father, brothers and Potiphar's wife); gatekeepers (Potiphar, keeper of the prison, and the Butler) and divine helpers (Pharaoh and all the destiny helpers, and gate-keepers mentioned above).

Please do not think that people who are to help you reach your destiny will always have good intentions for you. Some of the people that you come across will cause you great harm, attack you, envy you and intend evil for you. However, be like Joseph. Do not be weary in doing good, for God has a purpose for your life.

See Genesis 50:20:

"You meant it for evil, but God meant it for good."

In the book of Galatians 6:9, we learn that we should not grow weary of doing good, for, in due season, we will reap if we do not lose heart.

The woman in our story (2 Kings 4) identified the prophet as the one that could help, and she received help. She had identified her divine helper; she was not disappointed.

So, the third set of questions you need to ask yourself in your journey to true financial triumph are:

- Do I know who my divine helpers are?
- Have I prayed specifically to God about this matter?
- Moreover, like Joseph, would I be ready to deliver when my name is dropped in the hearing of my gatekeeper?

PRINCIPLE 4

YOU MUST KNOW HOW TO CRY OUT

Note that not only did this widow know who she was, she had also assessed her position, identified her divine helper and knew how to cry out for help. She refused to bury her head in the sand; neither did she consider how the prophet would react.

You must know how to cry out for help, once you realise you need help. The measure of your shouting is the measure of your problem.

Chapter 1: Spiritual Building Blocks

Psalm 34:4 says,

> "For I sought the Lord and He heard me and saved me from all my problems."

Moreover, the measure of your crying out will be the measure of the response you get. By crying out and seeking, David was drawn out of his troubles.

Psalm 34:6 says,

> 'This poor man cried out, and the Lord heard him, and saved him out of all his troubles."

Let's look at some other examples in the Bible of individuals who sought the Lord:

- Nehemiah 1:1-6. By the time Nehemiah got to this stage of crying, he had fulfilled the three other steps - He knew who he was; he had taken a self-assessment of Israel, he knew whom to cry to, and he knew how to cry.

    > "It came to pass in the month of Chislev, in the twentieth year, as I was in Shushan [a] the citadel, that Hanani one of my brethren came with men from Judah; and I asked them concerning the Jews who had escaped, who had survived the captivity, and concerning Jerusalem. And they said to me, "The survivors who are left from the captivity in the province are there in great distress and reproach. The wall of Jerusalem is also broken down, and its gates are burned with fire." So it was, when I heard these words that I sat down and wept, and mourned for many days; I was fasting and praying before the God

> *of heaven. And I said: "I pray, Lord God of heaven, O great and awesome God, You who keep Your covenant and mercy with those who love You and observe Your commandments, please let Your ear be attentive and Your eyes open, that You may hear the prayer of Your servant which I pray before You now, day and night, for the children of Israel Your servants, and confess the sins of the children of Israel which we have sinned against You. Both my father's house and I have sinned."*

- In Daniel's case, we see the same pattern. Daniel was sure of who he was. He had a clear pathway of always knowing whom to cry to and Daniel, (then in activating this third principle), sought the Lord through fervent prayers and fasting (Daniel 2:18-19 and Daniel 9:3-4). These were desperate periods in Daniel's life. The first was when King Nebuchadnezzar wanted someone to tell him his dream and then interpret it - a difficult challenge indeed! The second was when Daniel discovered that the time for the children of Israel to be in slavery had passed. See Daniel 9:2-3,

> *'The first year of Darius the son of Ahasuerus, of Median descent, who was made king over the kingdom of the Chaldeans - in the first year of his reign, I, Daniel, observed in the books the number of the years which was revealed as the word of the LORD to Jeremiah the prophet for the completion of the desolations of Jerusalem, namely, seventy years. So I gave my attention to the Lord God to seek Him by*

Chapter 1: Spiritual Building Blocks

> *prayer and supplications, with fasting, sackcloth, and ashes."*

- Some of the great miracles in the New Testament all involved elements of "seeking the Lord," which is a distinct requirement for financial triumph. The Bible teaches us in Matthew 7:7-8 that we should ask, and we shall receive. Even though God is all seeing and all knowing, He still requires that we ask Him and seek Him. In John 5, Jesus asked the man at the pool of Bethesda: "Do you want to be well? Go ahead and ask for help." It is no time to be ashamed.

This is not a book of prayers, but it is important that we understand the different types of asking. It is not necessarily limited to a time of physical shouting. It could be in a variety of ways mentioned in the scriptures above.

Prayers should be from the soul, for example, Hannah's cry in 1 Samuel 1:10,

> *"And she was in bitterness of soul, and prayed to the Lord and wept in anguish."*

It could be by a "fasting that pleases God," see Isaiah 58:

> *"'Cry aloud, spare not; Lift up your voice like a trumpet; Tell My people their transgression, and the house of Jacob their sins. Yet they seek Me daily, And delight to know My ways, As a nation that did righteousness. And did not forsake the ordinance of their God. They ask of Me the ordinances of justice; They take delight in approaching God. 'Why have we*

fasted,' they say, 'and You have not seen? Why have we afflicted our souls, and You take no notice? "In fact, in the day of your fast you find pleasure, and exploit all your labourers. Indeed you fast for strife and debate, And to strike with the fist of wickedness. You will not fast as you do this day, to make your voice heard on high. Is it a fast that I have chosen, a day for a man to afflict his soul? Is it to bow down his head like a bulrush, and to spread out sackcloth and ashes would you call this a fast, and an acceptable day to the Lord? "Is this not the fast that I have chosen: to loose the bonds of wickedness, to undo the heavy burdens, to let the oppressed go free, and that you break every yoke?"'.

It could also be through meditation, and by any other means, but it must be directed at the Lord and a cry for help.

The other thing that we must know is that we must ask and cry out in faith. James 1:5-8 says,

"If any of you lacks wisdom, let him ask of God, who gives to all liberally and without reproach, and it will be given to him. But let him ask in faith, with no doubting, for he who doubts is like a wave of the sea driven and tossed by the wind. For let not that man suppose that he will receive anything from the Lord; he is a double-minded man, unstable in all his ways."

Hebrew 11:6 says,

"But without faith, it is impossible to please Him, for he who comes to God must believe that He is,

Chapter 1: Spiritual Building Blocks

and that He is a rewarder of those who diligently seek Him."

Also, in James 4:3, we read,

"You ask and do not receive, because you ask amiss, that you may spend it on your pleasures."

From the above verses, it is clear that the reason why our prayers are sometimes not answered is that we are asking with wrong motives, for example, we want God to prosper us so that we may spend it on our pleasures. When we ask, it is important that we believe that we will receive but, remember that the objectives of our asking should always be to meet our needs, fulfil His covenant and glorify the Lord. See Deuteronomy 8:18,

"And you shall remember the Lord your God, for it is He who gives you power to get wealth, that He may establish His covenant which He swore to your fathers, as it is this day."

So, the fourth question you need to ask yourself in your journey to true financial triumph is "Have I cried out to my Source, the Almighty God?"

PRINCIPLE 5

YOU MUST BELIEVE THAT THE ONE YOU HAVE CALLED ON CAN HELP/ANSWER YOU.

We must have an assurance that the One we have called on is able and willing to help. The willingness of

God to reward us is based on the covenant we have with Him. We see this in many passages of the scriptures, including Ephesians 1:3-4:

> *"Praise be to the God and Father of our Lord Jesus Christ, who has blessed us in the heavenly realms with every spiritual blessing in Christ. For he chose us in him before the creation of the world to be holy and blameless in his sight. God Himself has blessed us in heavenly realms with every spiritual blessing in Christ Jesus, for He has chosen us even before the creation of the world."*

Again, we see God's assurance of His promises in Galatians 3:13-14,

> *"Christ hath redeemed us from the curse of the law, being made a curse for us: for it is written, Cursed is every one that hangeth on a tree: that the blessing of Abraham might come on the Gentiles through Jesus Christ; that we might receive the promise of the Spirit through faith."*

Genesis 1:28 provides another example,

> *"And God blessed them, and God said unto them, be fruitful, and multiply, and replenish the earth, and subdue it: and have dominion over the fish of the sea, and over the fowl of the air, and over every living thing that moveth upon the earth."*

Also, remember that He rewards those who diligently seek Him. When you trust and believe in someone, you are not afraid or tired or weary of going to them every

Chapter 1: Spiritual Building Blocks

time the need arises. It is just like your child warning a bully to be careful because he has a father who can be called on to deal with the bully. Your child does not look at how big, muscled, large or fearsome the bully is compared to you; he just has a sound assurance that his father can surmount any bully.

Now that we have considered the five good things that we need to do as demonstrated by the prophet's wife, let's consider what this family (including the late prophet himself) did not do:

1. LACK OF PREPARATION

Preparation tells us of a surety that we can benefit. "Because we know that when preparation meets opportunity, breakthrough happens" - Timothy Kolade.

In 2 Kings 4, we find out that this woman believed she had nothing to offer, she was not prepared to take the victory; she was merely looking for someone to wave a magic wand and make things go away. She had not considered her potentials.

Many of us today think like this woman did. We are unprepared for the position God has in store for us. We are overwhelmed with the issues in our life and have not given thought to those abilities within us that may lead to our victories.

The prophet's question in 2 King 4:2 was a call for this woman to reflect on her potentials. Elisha response to her cry was, "How can I help you? Tell me, what do you have in your house?" Elisha was saying to her, "have you searched within, have you considered what you have in your house; and what you can do with this?" The woman was not prepared. She failed in the area of preparation. Many people are not ready for success. If you think deeply, God will reveal to you, areas of strength that can cause a breakthrough in your life.

Many of us have incredible gifts inside of us, but we are not thinking enough. Such gifts include having a flair for writing, cooking, and beauty and fashion techniques. Often our gifts just need to be deployed and commercialised to make us financially successful. Many of us are afraid to commercialise the gifts inside of us. You cannot make big money from a salaried income. If that is your ambition, there is always going to be a limit.

The woman was so overwhelmed with being a full-time housewife that she did not think of making money by trading what she had. She did not prepare herself for financial breakthrough. She never for once thought that she could find herself in this mess as her husband had everything going for him. She did not know the power of what she possessed. A woman, who wants to experience financial breakthrough at the level we are talking about, cannot be a full-time housewife alone. To be honest, being

Chapter 1: Spiritual Building Blocks

a full-time housewife is equally, if not more, than full-time work.

As a matter of fact and law, many women who get paid big money after divorces tend to show their full-time house chores and looking after children as reasons why they deserve equal payouts. I agree. However, I think this woman found comfort being the Pastor's wife. She was not seeking until she had to!

"Those who seek The Lord shall not lack any good thing" (Psalm 34:10).

Don't get me wrong; it is a wonderful honour to be a Pastor's wife as long as you can meet your needs from your husband's earnings. What I am teaching in this book, however, is for those who want to obtain exponential wealth to be able to fulfil some divine covenants that go beyond the ordinary.

God can bless your 9am-5pm job, and I accept and respect that not everyone is cut out for business. Some are career minded, while others are entrepreneurs. However, if you want wealth that will bring satisfaction and comfort beyond the ordinary, then consider some form of business.

It is my opinion that combining a 9am-5pm job with another business for a long time is not okay. Eventually, you would not give either of them the attention each requires for the optimal standard. You probably end up using your employer's time to make money. I think, you can do what some refer to as 9am-5pm-9pm. Do your salaried work from 9am-5pm, and start your work from 5pm-9pm.

However, can you last with this work schedule? I discovered I could not help when in those days I was combining my consultancy firm with working full-time for a law center. I resigned and took my fate in my hands. I flourished because I could now dedicate my full time to my own business.

Let's return to our previous discussion – that the ability to think and prepare, reside in us and that God has given us the power to make wealth (Deuteronomy 8:18). Think, and you would be amazed how much you have hidden in you.

When you are fully prepared, then you can withstand any question. The woman would have been able to answer the prophet when she was asked. "What do you have in your house?" In Job 38:3 and Job 40:7 we are told *'Now prepare yourself like a man, I will question you, and you shall answer'* I find many people come to me with a business idea. I ask them, tell me about your business? Alternatively, where is your business plan or strategy? So many times, they are dumbfounded. You cannot start your own business if you cannot master it and put it in writing. It is your idea; you cannot sell it if you do not

Chapter 1: Spiritual Building Blocks

know it. Job 13:18 says 'See now, I have prepared my case, I know that I shall be vindicated.'

I believe one of the hallmarks of a prepared mind, is a ready mind. Habakkuk 1:1-4 (NLT) makes it clear and apt. 'I will climb up to my watchtower and stand at my guard post. There I will wait to see what the Lord says and how he will answer my complaint. The Lord said to me, write my answer plainly on tablets so that a runner can carry the correct message to others. The vision is for a future, it describes the end, and it will be fulfilled.'

It is evident from the above that until we are prepared and ready, the message cannot come, the fulfilment cannot come.

I believe the reason why the woman had oil was that in those days they use a lot of anointing oil, especially in a prophet's house. However, she could not see the power in what she was familiar with. God will bless you with what you have in your hands. As we can see in Psalm 90:16-17,

> "Let Your work appear to Your servants, And Your glory to their children. And let the beauty of the Lord our God be upon us, and establish the work of our hands for us; Yes, establish the work of our hands."
>
> Do not make a toy out of your talent! - Timothy Kolade

2. LACK OF FORWARD THINKING ABILITY

The dead prophet did not engage in forward thinking. This is similar to the above but with a slight outcome. He failed to consider what may happen to his family in his absence. Furthermore, it will seem that his sons (unless they were too young) had no trade, no education and were unskilled for life. Hence, he had also failed to prepare them for life. We know this because the sons were going to be taking as slaves. They were not fit for purpose in employment or business. This act in itself is a major flaw for the prophet and one that many Christians fall into. Not only does it put the family at huge risk of a financial crisis, but it also brings about a questioning of the individual's character. We shall explore this further in the next chapter.

Food for thought: How long do you have more to work before you retire! How old would you be in 20 years, and what would you be doing?

Chapter 2

Character Building

There are many ways in which we could choose to prepare for financial triumph. In this chapter, we will focus on financial triumph through character building and the key character we will concentrate on is integrity.

WHAT IS INTEGRITY?

The dictionary definition of integrity is 'an unimpaired condition, that is, soundness, wholeness, firm adherence to a code of moral values.' For example, incorruptible, honour, the quality or state of being complete or undivided, that is, completeness. Synonyms of integrity are honesty and unity.

The first question to ask ourselves in building our character up for financial triumph is "What grade will God give my level of integrity?"

Let's pause for a moment to consider one of the main characters in our story- the deceased prophet. It will be safe to state that he failed to build a well-rounded character as forward thinking was not part of his character traits.

By not considering the future, he placed himself in a position where his integrity towards his family was called into question. We know this because a man of integrity would not have left debts for his family to the point of his sons being at the mercy of creditors. We may think that this is a harsh statement to make, but it is a true one. He lacked integrity in keeping to the standards set by God for us. God's plan for man, right from the time God created the first man was for the man to be blessed, be the head of the home and be the provider. This places upon him (the man) the responsibility of providing for his household. The Bible says,

> *"But if any provide not for his own, and especially for those of his own house, he has denied the faith and is worse than an infidel" (1 Timothy 5:8).*

By God's arrangement, the husband is to provide for his family. He is the one who must ensure there is food for members of his family. He must make sure his family members are well taken care of, especially his immediate family members.

The prophet was as the man referred to in Song of Solomon 1:6,

> *"Don't stare at me because I am dark - the sun has darkened my skin. My brothers were angry with me;*

Chapter 2: Character Building

they forced me to care for their vineyards so that I couldn't care for myself - my own vineyard."

We do not know the reason why the dead prophet was not able to provide for his family, but his situation was bad and was not one that aligned to the promises of God for his family. However, we do know from the story that he did do a few things right. He was a son of God; he stayed in ministry and served God under the leadership of a prophet. He remained married and had small savings (oil).

The Bible goes to great lengths to highlight the importance of integrity, see 2 Peter 3:11, Proverbs 10:22; Genesis 26:14; Job 1:1-3 and Matthew 5:48. The question to ask yourself is: "what will I score and how would God mark me on my integrity?" God provides an answer to this question and a clear path for us to follow in Matthew 6:33, which says,

"Seek ye first the Kingdom and His righteousness and every other thing shall be added unto you."

This statement in itself defines how God will judge our integrity. God expects us to seek His kingdom and His righteousness first and in the quest for this, He states that all other things get added to us including eternal life which is the essence of our life.

Righteousness does not mean that we do not have errors of judgment, it means seeking after the mind of

God and ensuring your intentions are not selfish. Look at Psalms 5:12 which says,

> *"For You, O Lord will bless the righteous; with favour. You will surround him as with a shield."*

This verse defines the joy of righteousness. 2 Timothy 2:22 also teaches us to pursue righteousness. Righteousness comes from the heart, check your motives for your actions or the reasons you want God to bless you. If your heart is not right, you cannot have a good relationship or a solid foundation with God. Your heart must be right to receive the favour of God. Again, let's look at Romans 10:5-6,

> *"For Moses writes about the righteousness which is of the law, 'The man who does those things shall live by them.' But the righteousness of faith speaks in this way, Do not say in your heart, 'Who will ascend into heaven?' (that is, to bring Christ down from above)."*

This approach to righteousness serves as the basis for integrity. In 2 Peter 3:10-14, we read of the type of people God expects us to be and the rationale for that:

> *"But the day of the Lord will come like a thief. The heavens will disappear with a roar; the elements will be destroyed by fire, and the earth and everything done in it will be laid bare. Since everything will be destroyed in this way, what kind of people ought you to be? You ought to live holy and godly lives as you look forward to the day of God and speed its coming. That day will bring about the destruction of the*

heavens by fire, and the elements will melt in the heat. But in keeping with his promise we are looking forward to a new heaven and a new earth, where righteousness dwells. So then, dear friends, since you are looking forward to this, make every effort to be found spotless, blameless and at peace with him."

This is the picture of integrity that God sets for us. We must remember that if at the time we do not have wealth, and still do not seek to operate in integrity, then it is unlikely that we will experience a financial breakthrough. Remember Matthew 6:33 states,

"But seek first the kingdom of God and His righteousness, and all these things shall be added to you."

Also see Isaiah 1:19,

"If you are willing and obedient, you shall eat the good of the land."

Moreover, if in wealth we decide not to operate in integrity, we must realise that God will hold us accountable at His coming. 2 Peter 3:10 says,

"But the day of the Lord will come as a thief in the night, in which the heavens will pass away with a great noise, and the elements will melt with fervent heat; both the earth and the works that are in it will be burned up."

Also see Job 36:11,

> "If they obey and serve Him, They shall spend their days in prosperity, and their years in pleasures."

As explained in 1 Chronicles 29:17, Psalm 7:8, the Lord will test and judge your integrity,

> "I know also, my God, that You test the heart and have pleasure in uprightness. As for me, in the uprightness of my heart I have willingly offered all these things; and now with joy, I have seen Your people, who are present here to offer willingly to You" (1 Chronicles 29:17).

> "The Lord shall judge the peoples; Judge me, O Lord, according to my righteousness, And according to my integrity within me" (Psalm 7:8).

We will not carry our riches when we stand before God; therefore make sure you are standing before Him with integrity and not in shame.

Integrity is, therefore, one of the first points of call for any serious minded Christian seeking for financial triumph. Integrity in our relationships, homes, and ministry and in everything we do.

A son or daughter of God seeking for a financial triumph must have a character CV that reads like this (Bishop David Abioye):

- I am a person of integrity;

Chapter 2: Character Building

- I fulfil my promises regardless of it coming at a cost (Exodus 8:28-32)
- I am a person of sincerity, and I shun hypocrisy. I treat people fairly and honestly.
- I live by Leviticus 19:35-36 which states, You shall do no injustice in judgment, in the measurement of length, weight, or volume. You shall have honest scales, honest weights, an honest ephah, and an honest hin: I am the Lord your God, who brought you out of the land of Egypt.
- I also live by Deuteronomy 25:15, Proverbs 16:11-13.
- I maintain a wholeness of character, including kindness, compassion, mercy, and gentleness.
- I abide by God's laws.
- I play by the rules, both in the Bible and the law of the land.
- I have high levels of consistency regarding my behaviour, and I love the Lord.

Our integrity should set an example, see Titus 2:7-8,

"In all things showing thyself a pattern of good works: in doctrine showing incorruptness, gravity, sincerity, sound speech, that cannot be condemned; that he that

is of the contrary part may be ashamed, having no evil thing to say of you."

BENEFITS OF OPERATING IN INTEGRITY

The Bible makes it clear that integrity will be rewarded. For example, see 1 Kings 9:4-5:

> *"Now if you walk before Me as your father David walked, in integrity of heart and in uprightness, to do according to all that I have commanded you, and if you keep My statutes and My judgments, then I will establish the throne of your kingdom over Israel forever, as I promised David your father, saying, 'You shall not fail to have a man on the throne of Israel"*

Four such benefits include:

1. FAVOUR

Integrity triggers God's favour

> *"Surely, Lord, you bless the righteous; you surround them with your favour as with a shield" (Psalm 5:12).*

You will operate in favour and favour is one of the key openers to financial triumph. Also see Proverbs 16:17; 3 John 1:2. However, you will run out of God's favour when your heart is not right (Titus 1:15). Esther was favoured by man and God (see Esther 2:15-17 and see also Romans 10:10-11).

2. PROMOTION

Integrity brings about God's promotion (see Proverbs 14:34 and Psalm 75:6-7). As we walk in integrity and God's righteousness, He will promote us. Both Daniel and Joseph experienced promotion through integrity. Of Daniel, the Bible says,

> *"Then the other administrators and high officers began searching for some fault in the way Daniel was handling government affairs, but they couldn't find anything to criticize or condemn. He was faithful, always responsible, and completely trustworthy."*

Of Joseph, we notice his reasoning in Genesis 39:9. When his integrity was tested, he said,

> *"How then can I do this great wickedness, and sin against God?"*

No wonder God chose to promote both men.

3. DEFENCE

As we walk in God's righteousness and integrity, God places special grace on us and sets a defence up for our business, our family and all that surround us. Through character building of integrity, we enter into a partnership of less sweat and more gain. Psalm 127 says, 'except the Lord builds the house; they labour in vain that builds it, and except the Lord watches over the city, the watchman watches in vain.' In Genesis 30, we see God's protection over Jacob in the house of Laban. Because Jacob chose to practice integrity, God stood by him and defended him.

4. HONOUR

One of the important lessons to learn is the description of what wealth is in the eyes of God. To help us understand this, I will tell a story of an American missionary I once heard of. Having been on a missionary trip and having laboured so hard for God, he was on his way back to America. On the same ship was the President of the United States of America. He wondered, and questioned God about the reception that was being offered the President on the ship; the guards that were there to protect him, people to honour him and every pomp and wild celebration that he was being honoured with.

The missionary felt low and cried out to the Lord; he could not understand why he was not being celebrated; and in his state of desperation, God reminded him of the future, a day when he will be celebrated not by mere men but by God's angels. God reminded him of his account in heaven, and the fact that he was rich in eternal things; the things that mattered the most. As a Christian, we must have a full understanding of what financial triumph is and seek for it not just in this age but in the age to come. Integrity is the bedrock for this (Luke 18:29).

Chapter 2: Character Building

Ultimately, it is not about what we get when we pray in the name of Jesus but what we get when we have Jesus. All the material things are important, but they do not compare with having Jesus first.

God described and inputted eternal blessings and honour to this missionary because he had shown integrity in the work of God.

God will announce you as His child once you enter a certain circle as long as you are operating in His integrity, He will bless and distinguish you from your peers and those around you. In Genesis 26:10, we see Isaac in a land of famine being distinguished and honoured by God even during that national crises. Let's examine Genesis 26:10 onwards about this,

> *"Isaac sowed in that land and reaped in the same year a hundredfold. And the LORD blessed him, and the man became rich, and continued to grow richer until he became very wealthy".*

God's hand was on Isaac for blessings because he sowed with integrity.

Another example is Job; a man of integrity according to God Himself. Despite the hardships he experienced, when his wife asked him to give up on God (Job 2:9), he refused, and he stood for God. In Job 1:9, God lauded him to the Devil. In line with this, Proverbs 10:7 tells us that the memory of the righteous is blessed, that is they have a good reputation. For example, Enoch, that ancient Biblical personality has a memory that is blessed today because he operated in integrity. See Genesis 5:24,

> Enoch walked with God, and he was not, for God took him.

See also Nehemiah 7:2 which explains that Nehemiah appointed his leaders based on their integrity.

> *"I put in charge of Jerusalem my brother Hanani, along with Hananiah the commander of the citadel, because he was a man of integrity and feared God more than most people do."*

In Psalm 41:11-12, we can see that David had an assurance of his relationship with God based on his integrity.

> *"By this I know that You are well pleased with me, Because my enemy does not triumph over me.12 As for me, You uphold me in my integrity, and set me before Your face forever."*

Moreover, Abraham, the father of faith, operated in integrity and God called him His friend, James 2:23

The Scripture was fulfilled which says, "*And Abraham believed God, and it was reckoned to him as righteousness."* He was called the friend of God.

HOW DO WE COME INTO INTEGRITY?

No one was born into integrity or righteousness, and that is particularly relevant for many people who come to

Chapter 2: Character Building

know God in the middle of their lives. Other characters and ways of life may have been formed within us which all need to be realigned with the character traits God requires from us.

To come into the full and consistent manifestation of integrity, we need to go through a process of self-consciously unlearning bad behaviour and learning godly behaviour and integrity, all of which must be done by asking God to help us. The following actions will help us achieve this:

1. PRACTICE INTEGRITY

You can practice and exercise integrity, 2 Peter 1:5-7, For this very reason, applying your diligence [to the divine promises, make every effort] in [exercising] your faith to, develop moral excellence, and in moral excellence, knowledge (insight, understanding), and in your knowledge, self-control, and in your self-control, steadfastness, and in your steadfastness, godliness and in your godliness, brotherly affection, and in your brotherly affection, [develop Christian] love [that is, learn to seek the best for others unselfishly and to do things for their benefit].

The reason why we do not do things with integrity is that we are greedy and we want quick results. We must purpose in our hearts that we will not tell lies, we will not cheat. You can teach yourself to practice integrity. You can count to 10 before you speak. You can be careful about the things you say. You can develop self-control, patience, and endurance. These will help us to stay focused. There are some people we do business with but do not charge, not because we have not done that work but because we have chosen to sow a seed for a relationship or a bigger harvest in the future.

Many business people fail when it comes to sowing. Giving and sowing are acts of integrity. We can see how Isaac sowed and what it yielded for him, but we can sow a seed of integrity by giving in money, giving in time, giving in prayer. We can practice not to do bad things. We can train our minds and our thoughts, and the produce of our thoughts to always bring forth a good harvest. We can choose to be someone's confidant; they have told us something personal and sensitive to them which they do not want to be shared. We can decide not to share it and keep their secret. You can practice having a good family relationship with your spouse. There is nothing you choose to practice that you will not become a star in.

We see in Genesis 17:1 that Abraham was asked to be blameless. In Genesis 5:24, Enoch walked with God and God eventually simply took him to be with Him in Heaven. God also blessed Noah because of his integrity (see Genesis 6:9).

Chapter 2: Character Building

2. BE DETERMINED TO BE BLAMELESS

This means putting all your energy into the pursuance of behaviour that radiates God's will. As human beings, we will still make mistakes along the way no matter how hard we try to be good, that is what makes us human. We learn in such circumstances to rely on God's grace and mercy. Determine in your heart that you will pursue good. Find a Christ-fearing mentor to mentor you. There is a common saying that leaders take you where next you want to go; great leaders take you where you ought to be! A great leader holds the steering wheel with your hand and tells you where to steer the car (Deuteronomy 30:19). Moses advised the children of Israel to choose life, not death. He set the options before them, but he steered them towards life, not death. In Daniel 1:8, we see that Daniel, purported in his heart not to defile himself. His stance and determination were rewarded by God. Similarly, Jesus focused on the Cross, He determined in His heart to die to save the world:

Looking unto Jesus, the author and finisher of our faith, who for the joy that was set before Him endured the cross, despising the shame and has sat down at the right hand of the throne of God (Hebrews 12:2).

3. BE PERFECT AND COMPLETE IN ALL THINGS

Being perfect and complete means that you will not lack anything good (see James 1:4). If you have, you are satisfied; if you do not have, you are satisfied. Be self-sufficient with what God has blessed you with. Do not covet what other people have. As we know, this is one of the key points in the Ten Commandments as set out in Exodus 20:17,

> *"You shall not covet your neighbour's house; you shall not covet your neighbour's wife, nor his male servant, nor his female servant, nor his ox, nor his donkey, nor anything that is your neighbour's."*

Do not even take in your heart something that is not yours and God has ways of testing us to ensure that does not happen. Money is very often a source of such trials. The man who disciples me, once explained how his finances were attacked because of some inheritance but once that link was broken, he came into financial triumph.

When his mother died, he inherited a sum of money and properties. He simply accepted the inheritance and started using it. Unknown to him, the properties and money in the inheritance were cursed. He began to have financial problems over a period involving being unable to pay bills, only getting paid to do menial jobs and so forth. He then asked God what was wrong and God told him that He was the one behind the problems as he had cursed the inheritance.

I remember a Sunday Service in which I preached on the importance of integrity in financial matters. Immediately after the service, a family approached me

Chapter 2: Character Building

and gave me an amount of money because God had answered their prayers. The next day, I went to bank the money, I left the bank and just before getting into my car, I took a look at my receipt. I had been credited with £25,000 as opposed to £250! I immediately returned to the bank and informed the cashier; she was so relieved and grateful, and immediately made the correction. That was God testing me; the Devil was ready to accuse me for life if I did not return to the cashier. I could have said "Thank God! The wealth of the heathen is laid on for me!" However, would I ever share that testimony? How would I be able to face the cashier?

At another time, I was in Vienna, Austria, for a lawyer's conference. When the conference ended, I checked out of the hotel I was staying at. However, the check-out clerk billed me for what I did not take from the mini-bar, so I complained. She quickly adjusted the invoice and credited my account. However, that morning I had taken a bar of chocolate that she did not know about and was not on the invoice. I told her about it so she could correctly bill me. She thanked me and debited my account accordingly. I felt blessed because if an unbeliever (I am not sure of her faith) could credit my invoice without doubting, I would be a hypocrite to have taken what I did not pay for. That for me would be stealing.

Recently, I had a meeting with a lawyer of an opposite party in a matter I was involved with, at the Four Points by Sheraton in Lagos, Nigeria. I had ordered coffee at the bar. Somehow, I completely forgot to pay. I had another meeting after, and I left the place hurriedly and simply forgot. I had left the hotel when it suddenly occurred to me that I had not paid! I felt bad. I had to tell my driver to return to the hotel after having already driven about 2 hours away from the hotel. I walked up to the cashier and explained that I had returned to pay the bill. The barista was gob-smacked and was looking at me as if I dropped out of the sky!

I have included these stories as examples of seemingly insignificant situations that can stain your conscience for life and allow the Devil to mock your belief. Certainly, in times past, I would have just taken these instances for granted and not bothered to rectify them, but now, I know better.

4. LIVE BY WHAT IS GOOD

Matthew 7:12 states,

> *"Therefore, whatever you want men to do to you, do also to them, for this is the Law and the Prophets."*

Do things in such a way that God is glorified. Do not try to claim your right if it is going to cause offense. If asserting your right will bring God into disrepute, do not assert it. Operate based on a policy of peace and spotlessness. The all-powerful God will fight your battle for you. God fought the battle of the children of Israel in

Chapter 2: Character Building

the times of Esther. Haman conspired against the Jews, hoping to destroy them and take what belonged to them. Despite his promotion and the respect he had, (Esther 3:1-2), he was not satisfied. It was so bad that he advised the king of the reward and punishment due to one who did well and another who did evil. Mordecai and the Jews got the promotion he thought was due to himself, but he got the punishment that he thought was due to Mordecai and the Jews (Esther 3-7).

If you want to experience financial triumph, run and resist evil. You cannot sow mango and expect to reap oranges. I am yet to see someone who is in the habit of blocking another person's goodness and gets away with it. It may take time, but ultimately, nemesis would catch up.

For us to make our journey into a season of financial triumph, there is a need for us to examine our spiritual and physical capacity for financial triumph.

God's promises of financial breakthrough are all real; He will not change his mind or shift to another position because we doubt or are unprepared or lack integrity regarding planning. He is also a faithful God; when we meet ourselves in the position of lack or when we are not getting our financial triumph, we can call on Him, He is our higher authority. We can do exactly what the widow in 2 Kings 4 did because we qualify to be blessed.

In the corporate world, people with integrity stand tall and stand apart. Please find below, an article on integrity that I enjoyed reading:

9 TIPS TO STRENGTHEN INTEGRITY

Learn how to take the high ground—because integrity is a core value essential to trustworthiness.

If you ask company executives to reveal their "core values," integrity is always one of their first answers, says Joel C. Peterson, chairman of the board of JetBlue Airways and a Stanford University professor of management. The single most important ingredient to business success is trust, Peterson says, and trust starts with integrity (Robin Amster, January 17, 2015).

Entrepreneur and angel investor Amy Rees Anderson borrows from C.S. Lewis's famous quote, defining integrity as "doing the right thing all the time, even when no one is looking - especially when no one is looking."

Anderson offers many examples of acting without integrity: CEOs who overstate their projected earnings because they do not want to be replaced by their boards of directors. Competitors who lie to customers to seal a deal. Customer service reps covering up mistakes because they fear clients will leave. There's no shortage of high-profile major lapses, too: Bernie Madoff's long-standing operation of a Ponzi scheme considered to be the largest financial fraud in U.S. history, Michael Milken's

Chapter 2: Character Building

conviction for violating U.S. securities laws after being the one-time toast of Wall Street, and Major League Baseball star Alex Rodriguez' use of performance-enhancing drugs.

However, what does a person acting with integrity look like? Positive examples may be harder to find. Anderson, who lectures on entrepreneurship at the University of Utah, believes "there aren't enough of us saying that sometimes it is better to lose than to lose your integrity." A plaque in Anderson's office reinforces her philosophy: "Do what is right; let the consequences follow."

That holds true in both personal and professional relationships. "If you do not have integrity, it bleeds over into other parts of your life," she says. Peterson agrees, saying that integrity cannot be compartmentalised — that "there is a kind of integrity across all of our behaviours."...

As for building your integrity and modelling it for others, Simons, Peterson, and Anderson offer these suggestions:

1. **Fulfil your promises** to your staff, your investors, everyone. If you break a promise, you must apologize, but don't let this become a pattern.

2. **Keep appointments.** Doing so affects you professionally and personally (practicing your faith, staying fit, being present for family, etc.).

3. Before you make a commitment, "stop and soberly **reflect on whether you are 100 percent sure you can deliver**," says Simons. "You need to be dispassionate in that evaluation."
4. **Get comfortable with saying no.** No one can say yes to everything and follow through on it all.
5. **Examine how you react in knee-jerk situations,** as well as how you make longer-term commitments (e.g., attending events, completing projects, etc.). Use this introspection to become self-aware, keep score and improve. (You can also use this behavioural yardstick for determining whether others act with integrity.)
6. **Polish your communication skills.** Reread that email or report before you send it; plan what you'll say in oral presentations and phone calls. "Fuzzy communication leads to broken promises," says Simons. Ask someone to proofread written communications and point out ambiguities before you distribute them.
7. **Consider the habits and skills you need to develop to enhance your integrity.** You might need to stop certain actions (e.g., speaking impulsively or sugar-coating your responses). Moreover, you might need to improve on others: building your personal courage (because fear holds you back from acting with integrity — Peterson's

CFO might have been fired without others showing courage). Issue apologies "faster, simpler and aimed more at containing the damage [you may have done] than at justifying yourself," says Simons.

8. Peterson advises taking **great care with the language you use,** especially when dealing with sensitive issues such as sexual preference, racism, and religion.

9. **Avoid people who lack integrity.** "Do not do business with them," Anderson writes in a blog post. "Do not associate with them. Do not make excuses for them. It is important to realise that others pay attention to those you have chosen to associate with, and they will inevitably judge your character by the character of your friends."

GAUGING YOUR INTEGRITY

Do you act with integrity? You can make an accurate assessment by asking yourself these six questions devised by Don Phin, a lawyer, author and vice president of Strategic Business Solutions at the compliance and training solutions company ThinkHR:

1. Am I willing to say what I am thinking?
2. Am I willing to risk being wrong?

3. Do I want my child or someone else I love to do that? If not, then why am I doing it?
4. Does this conduct make me a better person?
5. Am I leading by example?
6. Am I taking 100 % responsibility?

FOOD FOR THOUGHT: Where in the Bible do we learn of being qualified to be blessed?

- We have been redeemed from the curse of the Law (Galatians 3:13-14).
- We have dominion over everything (Genesis 1:28).
- How He made us to be accepted in His Beloved (Ephesians 1:6).
- The ploughman will overtake the reaper and the treader of grapes those who sow seed (Amos 9:13).

What do you have within you? What has God given you regarding talents, gifts, and resources which you currently are overlooking but could be the source of great wealth for you? What is God's purpose for your life?

These will be explored in the next few chapters.

Chapter 3

Capacity Building - Purpose

In this chapter, we will be finding and developing capacity through purpose and also:

- Explore what 'purpose' is;
- Establish how to discern purpose;
- Examine why purpose is central to living and then,
- Show the alignment between purpose and financial triumph for a Christian.

DEFINING PURPOSE

To operate in financial triumph, we must understand the purpose of our being and work towards developing that purpose. To achieve this, we must each find out what it is God wants us to do.

Before we go on, it is important to clarify that apart from a specific purpose for your life and for creating your wealth, everyone has a general purpose to fulfil as a child of God. This general purpose includes righteous living, studying and obeying God's Word and winning souls for Christ.

In Luke 4:18, Jesus declared to the world what His purpose was. He said,

"The Spirit of the Lord is upon Me, because He has anointed Me To preach the gospel to the poor; He has sent Me to heal the brokenhearted, To proclaim liberty to the captives, And recovery of sight to the blind, To set at liberty those who are oppressed."

This verse clearly outlines the reason why Jesus came to the world. Jesus knew He was called. He knew He was chosen to destroy the devil (see 1 John 3:8) and to bring salvation to all men. Moreover, in John 19:30, as He hung on the Cross, Jesus declared "It is finished" as, by dying for humanity, the purpose for which He had been called had been accomplished.

The first chapter of the Book of Luke, Luke 1:29-38, sets out the discussion between Mary and the angel who foretold Jesus' birth. This discussion was about purpose. The angel announced Mary's purpose for that specific time and season. Understandably, Mary felt inadequate and unable to comprehend how this will be. We also see in these verses that the angel gave an assurance to Mary by stating that with God, nothing is impossible.

Chapter 3: Capacity Building - Purpose

WHAT THEN IS 'PURPOSE'?

Purpose is what you can do because God has commanded you to do it and you are at peace with it. It will usually be a specific word which has been spoken to you by God either directly, from the pulpit or through a prophet of God.

To help us understand purpose, let's take a look at the following scripture:

> *"The words of Jeremiah the son of Hilkiah, of the priests who were in Anathoth in the land of Benjamin, to whom the word of the Lord came in the days of Josiah the son of Amon, king of Judah, in the thirteenth year of his reign. It came also in the days of Jehoiakim the son of Josiah, king of Judah, until the end of the eleventh year of Zedekiah the son of Josiah, king of Judah, until the carrying away of Jerusalem captive in the fifth month. Then the word of the Lord came to me, saying: "Before I formed you in the womb I knew you; before you were born I sanctified you; I ordained you a prophet to the nations." Then said I: "Ah, Lord God! Behold, I cannot speak, for I am a youth." But the Lord said to me: "Do not say, 'I am a youth, 'For you shall go to all to whom I send you, and whatever I command you, you shall speak."*
> (Jeremiah 1:1-7)

Jeremiah was set apart; God had decided Jeremiah's purpose even before he was born. God sanctified him and ordained him before he was in the womb. Key points we can take from the above passage are:

- Jeremiah's purpose was specific, and it was tailored to him, and God Himself told Jeremiah what His purpose for him was.
- We, therefore, can conclude that purpose must be communicated to man from God, it must be clear and must be backed by the Holy Spirit.

DISCERNING PURPOSE

Four factors that can help you discern your purpose:

1. A TOTAL LACK OF SELF

If God is speaking to you, I advise you to forget about your will and commit to the instruction He is giving you. Anything you do in reliance on yourself means God is not in control.

Examples of Biblical figures who abandoned themselves to Christ include:

- Simon Peter, the theologians say was crucified upside down;
- John the beloved was exiled to the Isle of Patmos and put in a hot vat of oil but did not die; and
- Paul was beheaded; James was also beheaded.

These men forsook all and were willing to pay the ultimate price to fulfil their purpose (see Luke 5:11).

Chapter 3: Capacity Building - Purpose

So Jesus said to them, "Assuredly I say to you, that in the regeneration, when the Son of Man sits on the throne of His glory, you who have followed Me will also sit on twelve thrones, judging the twelve tribes of Israel" (Matthew 19:28).

2. A TOTAL DEPENDENCE ON GOD

God has a way of testing that we have and choose to have a total dependency on Him. With each test we pass, He moves us on to the next stage. As explained earlier, we must also bear in mind that except the Lord builds a house, anyone who tries to build it without God, is doing so uselessly. God requires, not some, but total and complete dependency on Him. God will test you, and when you pass, you will forever be successful.

3. AN ABILITY TO OBEY DIVINE COMMANDMENTS

This means that once you know a direction is from God, you promptly and completely obey. As is written in Lamentations 3: 37-38,

> *"Who has spoken and it came to pass, unless the Lord has commanded it? Is it not from the mouth of the Most High that good and bad come?"*

> *"I will instruct thee and teach thee in the way which thou shalt go: I will guide thee with mine eye. Be ye not as the horse, or as the mule, which has no understanding: whose mouth must be held in with bit and bridle, lest they come near unto thee" (Psalm 32:8-9).*

When God speaks to you and you heed that direction, you are living according to God's purpose because your 'walking' is based on His Word. In turn, the Holy Spirit backs and honours your obedience and the direction from God which you received.

4. BE SPIRITUALLY SENSITIVE AND WORK WITH GOD'S TIMING

During the three years of Jesus' earthly ministry, many people thought He was crazy. His brothers were embarrassed by Him and to save their reputation they told Him that He needed to go somewhere else and do His work. If He was unwilling to do that, they said to him to take action and stop doing His work in secret. They tried to convince Him it was time to show Himself and His works to the world. They wanted Jesus to try to impress the people with what He could do. He responded to them by saying,

"My time has not come yet" (John 7:6).

How many of us could show that type of self-control? If you could do the miracles that He could do and were being made fun of and challenged to show your stuff, what would you do? Would you wait until you knew that it was the right time sanctioned by God?

Chapter 3: Capacity Building - Purpose

A famous preacher once said,

- Whatever God cannot do in my life, let no man do it. When anyone offers you something you have prayed about, the first thing you ask is: God, are you the one that is behind this?
- Where God cannot take me, may I never reach there.
- What God cannot give me, may I never have.

In addition to learning how to know what our purpose is, we can also use the above passage to study the process of attaining the skills needed and developing ourselves for the purpose. We also need to be skilled in discerning what our purpose is. The specific verse to help with this is the statement made by God to Jeremiah,

> *"Before I formed you in the womb I knew you; before you were born I sanctified you; I ordained you a prophet to the nations" (Jeremiah 1:5).*

We can draw out the following five processes from this verse.

1) The process of hearing the word

> *God spoke and Jeremiah exercised his 'hearing.' Jeremiah must have been in a position of either waiting or in a position of being trained to hear and discern the voice of God. He knew the voice of the Lord and was able to clearly hear him speak. Compare this*

with the prophet Samuel. God first spoke to Samuel when he was a young boy. At that stage in his life, Samuel did not understand who was calling him until the fourth time, when the high priest, Eli, to whom Samuel was an assistant, had taught him how to respond when he heard God's call again (see 1 Samuel 3:4-10).

2) The process of forming

Before coming into your purpose, there is a process of forming. This might be learning, being set apart, being mentored or being tutored. We see examples of these in the Bible: Moses mentored Joshua, Samuel lived with Eli, Esther was guided by Mordecai and the disciples were led by Jesus. David was crowned king almost twenty years after he was anointed for the role and during those years he too went through a process of forming. Paul also went through this process (see Galatians 1:15 onwards). Please be aware that even Jesus was led by the Holy Spirit into the wilderness for forty days. Following this period, He confidently and clearly declared His purpose.

Arguably, the process of forming is when we address any areas of ignorance we have. It is a time of expanding our endurance; an opportunity of appreciating protocol and order. For some, it could be quick, for others, it could take several years. How long this process takes depends on each person's level of obedience to God.

Chapter 3: Capacity Building - Purpose

3) The process of being known or knowing

The process includes being honest with and understanding yourself. If you went through a spiritual appraisal, would you get the right ticks? Also, in this process, the Holy Spirit, through our mentors and disciplers, takes us through spiritual assessments. No one is entirely perfect as God keeps on perfecting us each day. However, when we realise that we have no strength of our own, then our gifts, purpose, and service will be unto God rather than unto ourselves or men. The knowing process requires us to be challenged, as it is only in being challenged that our true self is revealed. The calling of Samuel four times (by God that is) and Samuel going to Eli on three of these occasions is typical of the knowing process. Eli was able to carry out a spiritual appraisal and assess that God was the one calling Samuel. As for Samuel, we can clearly see the importance of hearing.

4) The process of sanctifying

This is the process of being set apart for a specific task. Jeremiah's task was specific, Mary's purpose was specific, Esther also had a specific purpose, and a study of her life reveals the process of sanctifying. Also, whenever the children of Israel took on a purpose of building or rebuilding, they always started this with a period of sanctification.

5) Coming into ordination

This is where recognition of your purpose or call is manifested. Let us consider Isaiah 43:7 which states,

> *"Everyone that is called by my name: whom I have created for my glory, I have formed him; yea, I have made him."*

This verse confirms that God calls (and as mentioned earlier, that is why we need the skill of hearing), God creates, forms and makes all for His glory.

We can draw out from this verse that the key reason for purpose is so that God can be glorified. God created humanity for His glory, for His purpose. Thus God's plan and purpose for us are always good and to bring Him glory. We see in Jeremiah 29:11,

> *"For I know the plans I have for you," declares the Lord, "plans to prosper you and not to harm you, plans to give you hope and a future."*

WHY IS PURPOSE CENTRAL TO LIVING?

Unfortunately, most people go through life without any concept or realisation of purpose.

People tend to live lives that are fully intended to fulfil only their desires. They strive to get all that is possible out of this life for their benefit, only to find that the gathering of the things of this world does not satisfy that profound and basic need for purpose.

Chapter 3: Capacity Building - Purpose

The reason for this frustration is simple. When we live a life for our purpose, we never accomplish anything greater than ourselves. However, when we understand that we were not created for our purpose but God's purpose, we find that we are designed to accomplish something far greater than ourselves: serving and glorifying the God who created us and in so doing we come into our financial triumph.

Going back to my definition of purpose, that is, 'whatever you can do because God had commanded you to do and you are at peace to do it; doing what you find easy to do in an extraordinary way.' Being in this position of the will of God for our lives can be imagined as being in a place where God reveals a master plan of the essence of life to you as an individual.

God gives the master plan and states to your hearing that this is what He wants you to do. From our earlier discussion, we understand that that comes through a process of hearing, forming, knowing, being sanctified and the ordaining or the doing, all of which are geared towards bringing glory to God.

Therefore, finding out what your purpose is and coming into your purpose can be compared to the action of building. Let's take a look at Psalm 127: 1-3 which says,

> *"Unless the Lord builds the house, they labour in vain who build it; unless the Lord guards the city, the watchman stays awake in vain. It is vain for you to*

rise up early, to sit up late, and to eat the bread of sorrows; for so He gives His beloved sleep. Behold, children are a heritage from the Lord, the fruit of the womb is a reward."

In light of the above verse, please understand that it is the action verb 'building' that is being discussed here. As in "building a God - given purpose." It could be a purpose connected to self, marriage, children, ministry or leadership.

Purpose once heard, formed, sanctified and recognised can be manifested in a place of building. It is manifested through building a particular thing that relates to what you can do because it is what God has commanded you to do and you are at peace with it.

Purpose can be manifested where you find yourself bringing out God's vision or where you find yourself in a place of supporting a group or a person or a cause. In such a place, purpose becomes the art and act of helping to build something that will glorify God. It could be your business, your ministry, your spouse, your family. That command of purpose will be unique to you for the purpose of building unto God's glory.

Your life will move in the direction of your most dominant thoughts Romans 12:2

The Lord can give you a purpose of building security. Some people want to help secure people and make them feel assured. Remember, if God is not building or watching over what you are building, you labour in vain (Psalm 127:1).

So what is the link between purpose and financial triumph?

The Lord can give you a purpose of glorifying Him through your business, through your role at work and your children. Very often, one of the ways purpose for financial triumph can come is, through our children. Also, as stated in the Bible, we must see our children as a heritage and reward from God (see Psalm 127:3).

I strongly advocate for a Christian to come into financial triumph through purpose.

If you meet the purpose of God for your life, you will be like Jacob. He worked for his uncle Laban for many years until he came to realise that the best he could get under Laban was a salary. He wanted more. In Genesis 30:25-30, he said to Laban,

> *"Let me go. ... And now, when shall I also provide for my own house?"*

There comes a time when what you earn as an employee is not enough to provide for your house.

When you work in the plan and purpose of God, no devil can touch you; you are untouchable. "[But] he who commits sin [who practices evildoing] is of the devil [takes his character from the evil one], for the devil has sinned (violated the divine law) from the beginning. The reason the Son of God was made manifest (visible) was to undo (destroy, loosen, and dissolve) the works of the devil [has done]" (1 John 3:8).

A 9 am to 5 pm career is very limiting (Please note this is with regards to being an entrepreneur. God uses us for many things in life. Be good in what you do). While God will make you comfortable and will supply your needs in the place of employment, using this, as a means for financial triumph is very often a challenge.

At the place of employment, when you plant seeds through the service you carry out, that is, the seeding, it is done for another individual's benefit, and the yield is based on wages. When at a place of your own business or creativity, the work of your hands and your gifts are seeds sown for yourself and the yielding gives you more seeds for sowing. The ultimate result is a great harvest.

However, please note that in running your own business, you are required to build and watch. Then, on average, with the right leading and direction by the Holy Spirit, a business will begin to yield following the first two years and begin to stand on its own in the next three to four years.

Chapter 3: Capacity Building - Purpose

HOW TO MAKE A REMARKABLE DIFFERENCE USING PURPOSE

1. DETERMINATION

Be determined. This is what drove Jesus to ignore the shame of the cross and to fulfil His destiny. When determination mixes with passion, an individual becomes unstoppable. The anointing through the Holy Spirit will bring time and chance, and the individual will be well prepared to step in.

> *"looking unto Jesus, the author, and finisher of our faith, who for the joy that was set before Him endured the cross, despising the shame, and has sat down at the right hand of the throne of God."* (Hebrews 12:2).

2. DISCIPLINE

To have discipline is to do what is required when required and within the boundaries of decency and legality. Daniel refused to eat of the palace food. He desired the godly food, and he received divine promotion and health, see Daniel 1:8: But Daniel purposed in his heart that he would not defile himself with the portion of the king's delicacies, nor with the wine which he drank; therefore he requested of the eunuchs that he might not defile himself.

Then look at Daniel 1:15,

> *"And at the end of ten days their features appeared better and fatter in flesh than all the young men who ate of the king's delicacies."*

3. SEEDING

As discussed in chapter 10 of this book, don't eat your seed; plant it, so that it can yield more fruit. Master the act of saving. Don't spend your capital foolishly. As set out in John 12:24,

> *"Most assuredly I say to you, unless a grain of wheat falls into the ground and dies, it remains alone; but if it dies; it produces much grain."*

4. DEDICATION

Be dedicated to your cause, follow through. Do not give up.

> *"But Jesus said to him, No one, having put his hand to the plow, and looking back, is fit for the kingdom of God"* (Luke 9:62).

5. ATTITUDE

A positive attitude to work and business is essential. Study the life of Jesus. He followed through in everything that He did.

Chapter 4

Capacity Building - Skills Development

In this chapter, I will be discussing skills development (the first part of Life Learning Building Block) and its role in wealth, wealth creation, and sustenance.

The world keeps changing; the certificate obtained at University twenty-six, thirty, forty years ago or even five years ago, is almost outdated and obsolete. If you have not improved it, I am sure it is outdated.

Those who can be dynamic with speed will get many things done and be rewarded by and large than those who are stagnant. People are diversifying into training, human development, and human capacity development. They are re-educating and re-orientating themselves. You find a medical doctor suddenly diversifying into advert production for radio stations. A medical doctor in Nigeria, I was told, with an exquisite voice is now into radio adverts. The ability to change, adapt and enhance your skills is what is probably going to take you out of poverty and set you on a good path to wealth creation.

The ability to harness, enhance and adapt your skills is a key means of creating wealth if you also have the grace of God. If you head a department and you are stagnant, your followers will know, and they will overtake you and have you removed. Nowadays, only those who enhance and adapt their skills retain their jobs for life. So the better skilled you are, the better your versatility, the quicker you will advance, and the wealthier and more comfortable you will be.

> *"The Proverbs of Solomon the son of David, king of Israel: "to know wisdom and instruction, to perceive the words of understanding, to receive the instruction of wisdom, justice, judgment, and equity; to give prudence to the simple, to the young man knowledge and discretion. A wise man will hear and increase learning, and a man of understanding will attain wise counsel, to understand a proverb and an enigma, the words of the wise and their riddles." (Proverbs 1:1-6).*

See also Daniel 5:10-12,

> *"The queen, because of the words of the king and his lords, came to the banquet hall. The queen spoke, saying, "O king, live forever! Do not let your thoughts trouble you, nor let your countenance change. 11 There is a man in your kingdom in whom is the Spirit of the Holy God. And in the days of your father, light and understanding and wisdom, like the wisdom of the gods, were found in him; and King Nebuchadnezzar your father — your father the king — made him chief of the magicians, astrologers, Chaldeans, and soothsayers."*

Chapter 4: Capacity Building - Skills Development

These four things are the essence of a fully civilised society:

1. Knowledge of wisdom and instruction;
2. Perception of words of understanding;
3. Reception of instruction of wisdom, justice, judgment, and equity; and
4. The handling of prudence to the simple (knowledge and discretion to the youth).

During World War II, Germany attacked the rest of Europe (the Allies) using coded messages sent to their troops. As the war progressed, the Allies tried to break the code so as to decipher the secret messages which were not written in ordinary words. Eventually, the Allies did hack the code, and thus Europe obtained an advantage over Germany. Deciphering the enigma gave the Allies power over Germany.

> *"The fear of the Lord is the beginning of wisdom but fools despise wisdom and instruction"* (Proverbs 1:7).

> *"But seek first the kingdom of God and His righteousness, and all these things shall be added to you"* (Matthew 6:33).

Anybody who is unable to acquire knowledge and adapt himself; anyone who is unable to concentrate on the statement of Proverbs 1:2-6 (as quoted above) should forget about acquiring and sustaining wealth. Consider what 1 Samuel 16:18 states about David,

> "Then one of the servants answered and said, 'Look, I have seen a son of Jesse the Bethlehemite, who is skilful in playing, a mighty man of valour, a man of war, prudent in speech, and a handsome person; and the Lord is with him.' Therefore Saul sent messengers to Jesse, and said, 'Send me your son David, who is with the sheep.'"

Look at all the skills David, a young man probably seventeen years old at the time, possessed. As long as you possess useful skills, your age is irrelevant. Even when you are not willing to move, your skills will move you to higher levels as David's skills did for him. For example, we know that Saul hired David into the palace because of his ability to play soothing music. David was promoted because of that skill. The Bible says,

> "Seeth a man diligent in his work, he will stand before kings and not mere men" (Proverbs 22:29).

Take a look at the British athlete, Mo Farah. Although undistinguished in earlier years, he became a success at the 2012 Olympic where his athletic skills distinguished him.

Your skills and the ability to maintain your skills will take you higher just as they did Joseph and Daniel.

In Daniel 5:11-12, although Daniel was captured alongside three other Hebrew boys, he was the only one taken to the palace in Babylon because he possessed a rare soft skill. Please be aware that your skills may take you away from your friends. All four boys went through

Chapter 4: Capacity Building - Skills Development

Babylonian assessment system and on passing, they were all taken to Babylon. Their skills took them that far, however, Daniel had the extra skill which was extraordinary. The more skilful you are, the higher you will go.

I know of a man who graduated from law school in Nigeria where I also graduated. He has since become a QC (Queen's Counsel) and a SAN (Senior Advocate of Nigeria). As a result of his skills and intelligence, he is now far ahead of some of us who were his contemporaries. It is not just because of intelligence, but he was able to harness his skills and his adaptability not only in Nigeria but also in Europe and the West.

At times, we have the knowledge, but we lack enthusiasm. We lack zeal and are too lazy rather than we do not know what to do. The likes of Mark Zuckerberg's (Facebook), Bill Gates (Microsoft), and Steve Jobs (Apple) of this world were/are always thirsty for knowledge. If I ask, since you left school, what new skill have you acquired and what short courses have you attended, the reply may be worrying. We use circumstances such as childcare (although good reason) to make excuses and other mundane reasons which tend (at times) to hold no water. As a child of God, we must run far away from the art and act of capitalising on any weakness. The focus for an individual seeking for financial triumph must be to stop talking about what you cannot do, why you cannot do it or what is preventing you from doing. An "If I had the opportunity or if my circumstances were different line," is irrelevant to victory,

You must not organise a pity-party session for yourself and don't expect a miracle! If what you live for is a miracle, there is a problem. Miracles very often come when things have gone wrong and as such, always expecting God to bail you out, does mean that you are putting no effort on your part. God does not like His children to live a life of excuses. See God's response to Moses excuse. Exodus 4:10-12,

> "Moses raised another objection to God: "Master, please, I don't talk well. I've never been good with words, neither before nor after you spoke to me. I stutter and stammer." God said, "And who do you think made the human mouth? And who makes some mute, some deaf, some sighted, some blind? Isn't it I, God? So, get going. I'll be right there with you — with your mouth! I'll be right there to teach you what to say."

Also God's response to Jeremiah, Jeremiah 1:6-8,

> "But I said, "Hold it, Master God! Look at me. I don't know anything. I'm only a boy!" God told me, "Don't say, 'I'm only a boy.' I'll tell you where to go and you'll go there. I'll tell you what to say and you'll say it. Don't be afraid of a soul. I'll be right there, looking after you." God's Decree.

Chapter 4: Capacity Building - Skills Development

If you are a parent reading this, you have to wake up and wake your children up. Perhaps, for us parents, it may be too late. Maybe not really; many people, who started very late in life, have made it exponentially. A good example is Colonel Harland Sanders who became a world-known figure by marketing his "finger lickin' good" Kentucky Fried Chicken.

The spectacled Colonel Sanders could easily be identified by his clean, crisp white suit, black string tie, and walking cane. A statue of this man can be seen as far away as on Nathan Road in Kowloon, Hong Kong, for one place.

One of the most amazing aspects of his life is the fact that when he reached the age of sixty-five, after running a restaurant for several years, Harland Sanders found himself penniless. He retired and received his first social security check which was for one hundred and five dollars. And that was just the beginning of his international fame and financial success story.

Col. Sanders was a fellow who loved to share his fried chicken recipe. He had a lot of positive influence from those who tasted the chicken. Now, the Colonel was retired and up in age and while most people believed in the sanctimony of retirement, the Colonel opted to sell the world on his cool new chicken recipe. With little, regarding means at his disposal, Colonel Sanders travelled door to door to houses and restaurants all over his local area. He wanted to partner with someone to help promote his chicken recipe. Needless to say, he was met with little enthusiasm.

He started travelling by car to different restaurants and cooked his fried chicken on the spot for restaurant owners. If the proprietor liked the chicken, they would enter into a handshake agreement to sell the Colonel's chicken. Legend has it that Colonel Sanders heard 1009 "no" before he heard his first "yes" (culled from an article written by Madelsa Singh in Team YS, 25th July 2012).

For our children, it is never too late. Some of them are still under thirty; some of them are 35. They have the language and understand the system. They have what it takes to possess the land. I love the Latin quote, "You possess, I possess, everyone possesses." With the opportunities our children have within their grasps, the sky is not even the limit.

> *"He teaches my hands to make war, so that my arms can bend a bow of bronze" (Psalm 18:34).*

That was David speaking. Do you submit yourself to teachings, because you do not know when things will happen?

God is a trainer and one of the areas he trains in, is warfare. By this, I am not suggesting that God will train you for mortal combat and guide you to join the British Army. I am referring to the type of war where there is a

Chapter 4: Capacity Building - Skills Development

struggle to take new territories or recover anything the Devil has stolen from your life.

John 10:10;

> *"The thief does not come except to steal, and to kill, and to destroy. I have come that they may have life, and that they may have it more abundantly."*

A man that will be successful at war must be prepared during the time of peace. You ought to be taught during peace time to succeed during war time. Unfortunately, many are too lazy to be trained. Nobody is going to shortlist you if your CV does not reflect any skill set. Your CV must be up to date and well presented.

At a recent speaking engagement for the ACS (African Caribbean Society) held at Warwick University, I was approached by a young woman working in one of the top UK companies. She explained to me how some children would never be employable at top blue chips companies because they did not go to universities within the Russell Group.

Russell Group universities are the British equivalent of the American Ivy League universities. I felt that she was unfair until she explained her reason. She said that those who attend those universities had already been trained and made ready for employment.

We need to prepare and teach our children how to be employable. It is our responsibility, and we must train them to be employable.

Look at David who was trained before he found himself in the palace. His training was in the form of the experience he gained.

> *"But David said to Saul, 'Your servant used to keep his father's sheep, and when a lion or a bear came and took a lamb out of the flock. I went out after it and struck it, and delivered the lamb from its mouth; and when it arose against me, I caught it by its beard, and struck and killed it. Your servant has killed both lion and bear; and this uncircumcised Philistine will be like one of them, seeing he has defied the armies of the living God.' Moreover David said, 'The Lord, who delivered me from the paw of the lion and from the paw of the bear, He will deliver me from the hand of this Philistine.' And Saul said to David, 'Go, and the Lord be with you!'" (1 Samuel 17:34-37).*

As you can see, David's experience and his training qualified him to be a general when other generals did nothing.

Stop investing in things that do not improve or enhance your status when you are still seeking employment such as expensive clothes, shoes, and watches. You can instead put your money in what will make you employable and when you are fully employable, you will be able to afford those things comfortably.

Chapter 4: Capacity Building - Skills Development

It is never too late, look at Abraham who started his life at the age of seventy-five. As far as I am concerned, the first seventy-five years of his life was a useless period. After seventy-five, he became somebody. There are people, who at a more matured age, changed their entire profession, retrained themselves and became successful, while there are young people who have given up on themselves. This is an absurdity. Improve yourself and become current. When you are current, the currency will be chasing you, pounds sterling, dollars, yen and so on.

You need to equip yourself for life. Do not tolerate lazy people who hide behind the label of housekeeping but indulge in watching meaningless TV soaps, dramas, and sitcoms. The producers of the popular television crime series, CSI: Crime Scene Investigation, are making loads of money while you waste your time watching it when you could be gainfully engaged. People spend valuable time discussing football transfers, while they are jobless. It is time for you to come to centre stage.

THREE WAYS TO DEVELOP SKILLS

1. LEARN TO STUDY

You must ensure that you know how to study. Develop a love for studying and do it. Also, develop your research skills. By studying and researching, you come across new knowledge, new ideas and you keep your mind brain. Imagine your brain to be a house, if you build a house and no one lives in it, it gathers dust and gradually, it depreciates. By the same token, if you pile up rubbish into your house, each time you enter the house, you are bound to meet your rubbish. So is the brain. The more you pile up useful materials through reading, studying and researching into your brain, the more you can withdraw from your "brain account" when you need to In Daniel 9:2, we can see how this very successful man also studied.

> *"In the first year of his reign I, Daniel, understood by the books the number of the years specified by the word of the Lord through Jeremiah the prophet, that He would accomplish seventy years in the desolations of Jerusalem."*

The desolations of Jerusalem concern the prophecies the Lord spoke through Jeremiah about how His people would remain in bondage and slavery for seventy years. At the point in Israel's history when Daniel was studying the books of the prophets, that period had been completed, and the Israelites were entering their seventy-first year of captivity. Through his reading and studying, Daniel realised the seventy years were up. If he did not read, they would have died in ignorance.

Until you are regularly updating your mind by reading or by acquiring knowledge, you will stay in ignorance and will be unaware of the advances being made in the world. There was once a man who went for a job interview that

Chapter 4: Capacity Building - Skills Development

he was very confident about. At his interview, he confirmed to the interviewer that he was computer literate. However, when he was given a task to accomplish on a new computer, he could not. His computer literacy was three years old and was outdated. He was rejected for the role.

Don't stagnate! Keep up to date with developments in your industry! Moreover, do not think that it is impossible. For example, I follow 24 hours News inside my head. American, British, Chinese, Nigerian news are all in my head. No news can go on for 24 hours without me being aware. I am aware of the location, what happened and what is being done about it. Moreover, my Bible reading is there, my silent therapy is there, my prayer is there, and I must still go to work. I have the ability to acquire knowledge round the clock. Moreover, thank God for our mobile phones and handsets. News with current information are readily and easily accessed on the go.

You do not have to feel insignificant or irrelevant. Know that you do not need a crowd to tap into your potentials.

By acquiring knowledge, you alone can liberate your generation and your nation from ignorance and servitude. That is what Daniel did.

2. ASSOCIATE WITH PEOPLE WHO LOVE TO LEARN

A second way to train is to associate with individuals who learn or who love to learn. Please note that this does not only refer to 'learned' people. Several highly successful people did not obtain a university degree. Learning and loving to learn refer to an attitude of the mind. Let us see 1 Samuel 22:1-3 which states,

> "David therefore departed from there and escaped to the cave of Adullam. So when his brothers and all his father's house heard it, they went down there to him. And everyone who was in distress, everyone who was in debt, and everyone who was discontented gathered to him. So he became captain over them. And there were about four hundred men with him. Then David went from there to Mizpah of Moab; and he said to the king of Moab, "Please let my father and mother come here with you, till I know what God will do for me."

Now, let us look at 2 Samuel 23:8-10,

> "These are the names of the mighty men whom David had: Josheb-Basshebeth the Tachmonite, chief among the captains He was called Adino the Eznite, because he had killed eight hundred men at one time. And after him was Eleazar the son of Dodo, the Ahohite, one of the three mighty men with David when they defied the Philistines who were gathered there for battle, and the men of Israel had retreated. He arose and attacked the Philistines until his hand was weary, and his hand stuck to the sword. The Lord brought about a great victory that day; and the people returned after him only to plunder."

Chapter 4: Capacity Building - Skills Development

From the first passage we read, they were miscreants, scoundrels, reprobates, and useless men, in debt and sleeping under the Adullam Bridge. However, by association with David, they became liberators of nations, and victorious. The people you associate with, are important. Your friends represent you. I have always loved to associate with individuals who are going somewhere. So if you are going somewhere good, I want to be with you.

An example of where bad company is picked up in the Bible as a recipe for disaster is in 1 King 12:5-16. This is the story of King Rehoboam. The people of Israel had brought him a challenge to help them resolve.

> *So he said to them, "Depart for three days, then come back to me." And the people departed. Then King Rehoboam consulted the elders who stood before his father Solomon while he still lived, and he said, "How do you advise me to answer these people?" And they spoke to him, saying, "If you will be a servant to these people today, and serve them, and answer them, and speak good words to them, then they will be your servants forever." But he rejected the advice which the elders had given him, and consulted the young men who had grown up with him, who stood before him. And he said to them, "What advice do you give? How should we answer this people who have spoken to me, saying, 'Lighten the yoke which your father put on us?" Then the young men who had grown up with him spoke to him, saying, "Thus you should speak to this people who have spoken to you, saying, 'Your father made our yoke heavy, but you make it lighter on*

us' — thus you shall say to them: 'My little finger shall be thicker than my father's waist! And now, whereas my father put a heavy yoke on you, I will add to your yoke; my father chastised you with whips, but I will chastise you with scourges!'" So Jeroboam and all the people came to Rehoboam the third day, as the king had directed, saying, "Come back to me the third day." Then the king answered the people roughly, and rejected the advice which the elders had given him; and he spoke to them according to the advice of the young men, saying, "My father made your yoke heavy, but I will add to your yoke; my father chastised you with whips, but I will chastise you with scourges!" So the king did not listen to the people; for the turn of events was from the Lord, that He might fulfil His word, which the Lord had spoken by Ahijah the Shilonite to Jeroboam the son of Nebat. Now when all Israel saw that the king did not listen to them, the people answered the king, saying "What share have we in David? We have no inheritance in the son of Jesse. To your tents, O Israel! Now, see to your own house, O David. So Israel departed to their tents.

This single incident of leaning on advice from bad company brought about the end of the reign of David's physical royal lineage in Israel. This single incident is very much still present today and even more especially in churches. Bad company is growing more and contributes to destroying the fabrics of the church when we should know better. People expose themselves to gossip, tale telling and story seeking, even more so by using so-called "spiritual channels" such as prayer partners, and counseling to fester bad company.

Chapter 4: Capacity Building - Skills Development

If you are truly seeking for financial triumph, your company of friends must be as to the standard stated by God, friends that will encourage you, tell you the truth and will add value to your life. People are afraid to gossip with me because they know that I will preach it out and direct them to discuss the matter in the presence of the named persons. People that I disciple or mentor know what it means to come to me with a story that does not add up. I will stand as a true friend and tell you exactly what you do not want to hear. This is the way to stop gossip and tell tales which are the foundational blocks to bad company.

I want to be in the company of intellectual talk. Some conversations on Facebook are ones that should not be associated with progressive minded people. The test for any serious minded person is to ask yourself, this person who is meant to be my "mentoring friend," am I comfortable and free with this person? Does this person allow for me to live a compromising average and unfulfilling life? If the answer is "yes," then be assured that that friend is helping you go nowhere and is not your friend.

We need to check our friends including our 'church friends'. A friend that is not going somewhere is a dangerous person. He is like a loose cannon rolling down from the top, not giving anyone any warning. When Peter was asked by Jesus whether he was going to join others that have left Him, Peter replied that he was going to stay because Jesus had the word of life. "We have associated with you, and we have seen you like life itself. We have burnt our bridges." They related to Jesus, and that association is what they are still benefitting from, till today.

Associate with those who will take you somewhere important.

3. KNOW WHO YOU ARE

The third way to train yourself is to be sure of who you are. You can check yourself. The widow of the prophet did not understand her status. In John 6:6, the Bible says Jesus already knew what He would do.

In John 2:5, the Bible says that Jesus' mother instructed the servants to do whatever He tells them to do because He has everything; knowledge, and understanding. Not only did Jesus know what to do; they were directing people to Him because He knew about life.

Take a minute now to mentally review your CV, the work that you do and the qualifications you have acquired. Compare that with the work you are currently doing now and see if they match. If you studied Chemistry, for example, are you anywhere near a laboratory (or the Lord has asked you to do something else)? It is time to ponder. Also, what is reflected in your bank account? Are you counting the zeros and asking

Chapter 4: Capacity Building - Skills Development

whom to blame? 'The society is to blame!' This is a very common and convenient reply.

God can liberate you from your current supposedly doomed position. It does not matter your age, education or personality, the grace of God is available. If you need strength and empowerment from God, or you are a bit confused or are not sure about where you should be, God can empower you. He can take you from where you are now to where you ought to be.

QUALITIES EVERY BUSINESS PERSON SHOULD POSSESS

> *"I have observed something else under the sun. The fastest runner doesn't always win the race, and the strongest warrior doesn't always win the battle. The wise sometimes go hungry, and the skilful are not necessarily wealthy. And those who are educated don't always lead successful lives. It is all decided by chance, by being in the right place at the right time"* (Ecclesiastes 9:11, MSG).

Although the common understanding of the above verse is that being in the right place at the right time outweighs individual merit, I encourage you to be open to what I am about to add. This scripture says more than what immediately meets the eye. I will want us to extend our revelation of this passage. It is true that God makes available to us divine positioning (time and chance). He makes available circumstances where His anointing comes forth for us.

Also, God can make you swift regardless of your circumstance. That is why an athlete might win a competition simply because God's grace was on him to be the winner for the day though he was competing with faster athletes. It is also customary for God to choose to ignore our strengths; He looks more at our hearts. God saw David's heart in 1 Samuel 16:7.

However, the Lord said to Samuel,

> *"Do not look at his appearance or his physical stature because I have refused him. For the Lord does not see as man sees; for man looks at the outward appearance, but the Lord looks at the heart."*

For that particular time, and season, David was God's man. It was Him who made David strong and bold for the purpose He has for him. 1 Samuel 17:54;

> *"And David took the head of the Philistine and brought it to Jerusalem, but he put his armor in his tent."*

However, as God connects us to time and chance, He expects us to have been fully prepared (Ecclesiastes 9:11). It is a two-sided coin, a partnership.

God wants us to be swift, strong (in Christ), have wisdom (in Christ), have understanding and also have skills. Every business person or professional must have these five qualities. Without these, an individual cannot make progress in their business or career.

Chapter 4: Capacity Building - Skills Development

Once these qualities are in place, we have fulfilled our part of the equation. God can then carry out the things only He can do, such as making time and chance happen to us. God very often and consistently play His part of the equation by bringing about time and chance. As we work together with God in this way, there will then be an outpouring of God's blessings and God will bring about profit to the work of our hands.

> *"And you shall remember the Lord your God, for it is He who gives you power to get wealth, that He may establish His covenant which He swore to your fathers, as it is this day" (Deuteronomy 8:18).*

By having these qualities, God shows His mercy. He will allow for time and chance to work for you and His anointing to breakthrough for you. Time and chance will only equal profit where these three qualities exist.

THE PROFIT EQUATION

Ecclesiastes 9:11 = Deuteronomy 8:18

God [time and Chance] + Man [swiftness, strong in Christ, Wisdom in Christ, understanding, and skills] (Ecclesiastes 9: 11) = Profit (Deuteronomy 8:18).

It is not the adjective that qualifies the man, rather, it is the man that qualifies the adjective.

4 THINGS EVERY BUSINESS PERSON MUST DO AND ACCEPT

1. GOD

The number one is God; you require God. We need to love and fear God. Believe in God, and you will be established. Daniel knew and believed in His God, and so he was able to do exploit.

"Those who do wickedly against the covenant he shall corrupt with flattery; but the people who know their God shall be strong, and carry out great exploits" Daniel 11:32.

2. SEE YOUR PASTOR AS YOUR PROPHET

Your pastor cares for your soul. He reveals the heart of God to you, through which you then grow into maturity and more believing and trusting relationship with God.

> *"Believe in the Lord your God, and you shall be established; believe His prophets, and you shall prosper"* (2 Chronicles 20:20b).

3. HAVE A FRIEND OR A PEER MENTOR

Create peer-to-peer power for encouragement and challenging each other to do more.

> *"And let us consider one another in order to stir up love and good works"* (Hebrews 10:24).

4. YOURSELF

You need to believe in yourself. Understand that God has given you everything that pertains to life and godliness.

> *"As His divine power has given to us all things that pertain to life and godliness, through the knowledge of Him who called us by glory and virtue" (2 Peter 1:3).*

> *"Now to Him who is able to do exceedingly abundantly above all that we ask or think, according to the power that works in us" (Ephesians 3:20).*

WEALTHY WAYS

Chapter 5

Breaking the Yoke of Poverty

In this chapter, we will examine how to break the yoke of poverty as a step towards financial triumph.

WHAT IS THE DEFINITION OF POVERTY?

Poverty is a curse; my personal definition of poverty is 'being in a situation or a position where one is not able to do what he needs to do, how it needs to be done, when it needs it done and for what it needs it done, in peace and health.' It is important to realise that the curse of poverty covers not just money it extends to peace and health. We must understand that though money is important; there are situations where people have money and are unable to spend that money because of their poor health or because of lack of peace. We see this very often with the rich, where despite having all the money, they still kill themselves.

Robert Williams was reported to have killed himself in New York City, USA. It was reported he had suffered a debilitating stroke in September 2015. Before his death, he was thought to have a personal fortune of about $800 million. He was 86 years old and his marriage of 35 years had also ended (Reported by Mail Online 16.10.2015).

It is, therefore, important for us to understand that if an individual has serious money, but on the day it is needed, is unable to spend that money because of ill health, because of troubles in marriage, trouble in business or at work, that individual is poor.

I do not want to dwell on poverty, but it is essential that as we understand the definition of poverty, we can also understand the yoke of poverty and how to break it.

Deuteronomy 28:15-68 onwards, gives a description of different kinds of curses and poverty. If you analyse them very well, you will see that they are mostly curses of lack, which come into operation when God's children refuse to obey the voice of God and to observe carefully all His commandments. You shall not be cursed in the mighty name of Jesus. Amen!

This scripture describes the yoke of poverty which also brings with it all the curses of the law. Moses explained and described these to the children of Israel, and he explained the fact that these curses would be the consequences of disobedience. These deadly consequences include:

Chapter 5: Breaking the Yoke of Poverty

1. The spirit of destruction;
2. The spirit of confusion; and
3. The spirit of slumbering.

1. THE SPIRIT OF DESTRUCTION

My prayer is as you read this book and as the anointed one of God, every spirit of destruction in your life will come to an end in Jesus' name. If we look at Proverbs 10:15, it says 'the rich man's wealth is his strong city and his defence. The destruction of the poor is their poverty'; it means poverty as a matter, of course, will bring destruction to the poor.

Who is the person that is poor? Someone that is not able to do what he needs to do, how he needs to do it, when he needs to do it, in peace and health is a poor man. I say you will not be a poor man from today in Jesus' name. Amen! The spirit of poverty is a devaluing agent, see Proverbs 19:7,

> "All the brothers of the poor hate him; how much more do his friends go far from him! He may pursue them with words, yet they abandon him."

That is why the man who is not able to do what he needs to do, how he needs to do it when he needs to do it and for what he needs to do it in peace and health, is cursed and is poor. For example, in a family meeting, they will say something like, "Who is asking for your opinion?" You are a poor man; if you cannot contribute to any event. If they go to buy something in the supermarket or by the roadside and cannot afford it, the people selling by the roadside will rain curses on such an individual. This is because the person is not able to do what he needs to do when he needs to do and for what he intended to do at that particular time. This is how poor people always have attracted curses. I say you will not be cursed in Jesus' name Amen!

The yoke of poverty brings with it physical death. See John 10:10 which says,

> *"The thief has come to steal, kill and destroy but God has come to give life and to give it more abundantly."*

Now there is an expansion of Proverbs 10:15 also in Deuteronomy 28:20. It says,

> *"The Lord will send on you cursing, confusion and rebuke in all that you set your hand to do until you are destroyed and until you perish quickly because of the wickedness of your doings in which you have forsaken me."*

2. THE SPIRIT OF CONFUSION

Confusion is an element of poverty, generally where poor people are confused as they do not know what to do and how to do it. If they do not have £10, they are confused because the £10 has suddenly become their god. They are confused about how they will send their

Chapter 5: Breaking the Yoke of Poverty

children to school, who will pay the tuition fees, how they will eat. A description of a poor family against the African setting is a picture of confusion. That is, a low-income family in the African setting is a family that finds it difficult to take decisions because their decisions are based on affordability rather than choice.

I advise you to pray to God, in Jesus' name, to destroy every spirit of confusion and poverty in your life. Pray that today, wherever you have been cursed, confused, wherever there is a rebuke, there shall be light in the mighty name of Jesus Amen.

Our hands are so special; the Lord has blessed our hands to perform great things. Psalm 90:16-17 says 'He will establish the works of our hands.' Every time the devourer comes against the blessings of our hands, it is the beginning of a sign of poverty. For some people no matter how they try in a particular type of business, it is when they come into the venture that things go bad. I say wherever you extend your hands; they will see the anointing of God in your life. Amen.

When Jacob, a seed of Abraham, was going to leave Laban, because of the anointing of God upon Jacob's life, Laban gave him an open cheque and begged for him to stay. He said ' I know since you came here God has blessed me; so he did not want him to go. Same thing with Joseph, wherever he went, he was favoured. His father loved him; Potiphar the warden loved him in prison. You as a seed of Abraham shall also receive favour in Jesus' name. I rebuke confusion and curses in your life in Jesus' name. These are the hallmarks that take the poor man into destruction.

3. THE SPIRIT OF SLUMBERING

The yoke of poverty comes with the spirit of slumbering, sleepiness, and sluggishness. It is the spirit of the Tsetse fly. The tsetse fly is a kind of fly that feeds on the blood of vertebrate animals and are primarily African biological vectors of trypanosomes which cause human sleeping sickness. See Proverbs 6:9-11,

> "How long will you lie there, you sluggard?" When will you get up from your sleep? A little sleep, a little slumber, a little folding of the hands to rest – and poverty will come on you like a thief and scarcity like an armed man. It is like a thief designed to take away breakthrough and joy from the lives of people."

The above verses ask for how long a lazy person sleeps. The spirit of slumbering is the spirit which is not able to do things at the time it ought to do it - when will you stop this slumbering oh sluggard. Some people suffer from the spirit of hazardous slumbering in their life. Everything they do even though they are fast, is slow. Even though it should come with abundance, it comes with lack. Pray that every spirit of the sluggard in your life today shall be terminated. The scripture is asking - when will you rise from your sleep?

Chapter 5: Breaking the Yoke of Poverty

This is an indication of a yoke of unconscious poverty; a state of amnesia, when you are not able to do what you should do to break that yoke. It is broken today in Jesus' name.

In this scripture found in Proverbs, King Solomon was concerned, that everybody could see that this man's life is going down the drain, but he could not see it. Everybody can see that he is always tired, losing weight badly, he is getting bigger badly, he is coming short, he is not prospering, but he is not able to see. He is blind and blinded.

In Genesis 1:3, God says let there be light, and there was light. Pray for God's light into your circumstances in Jesus' name. When you see an indication of poverty, and you see the yoke of poverty, you will see that there is a tendency to enjoy destructive sleep when you should be awake, there is a satanic tendency to be weak when you should be alert; that shall not be your portion in Jesus name. Amen!

Pray that every spirit that will put you to bed, when you should be fast awake working in your place of work and prospering in your business, disappear today in Jesus' name. It says a little sleep, a little slumber, a little folding of the hands to sleep. Do you know why some people say I just need a minute, let me just have a nap; I will wake up in five minutes. Just give me one minute? A minute never ends in their life? It is that spirit.

There are some people the Enemy has sent to perpetual sleep even though in the physical they are wide awake. It says a little folding of hands to sleep so shall your poverty come on you like a prowler and your need like an armed man. Many people who have become 'suicide bombers' as husbands or terrorists as I described it in my book "Make That Move Right Now" - 2008, do not know. They are not conscious of it. In many instances, such people are going down the drain, and when people are warning them, they will say no. The wife will say "we are drifting on this path you have embarked on, and it will lead us nowhere, we are going over the cliff, we have come to the precipice of our destruction," the man will not hear.

Pray that every destruction of the land is destroyed for our sake in Jesus name. Amen! How can we break free from the yoke of poverty? The good news is that once we become born again, we are not under the yoke of poverty. See 2 Corinthians 8:9,

> *"For you know the grace of our Lord Jesus Christ that though He was rich, yet for your sake He became poor, so that you through His poverty might become rich."*

Jesus humbled himself for our sake and had completed the work of releasing us from the yoke of poverty:

> *"And being found in appearance as a man, He humbled Himself by becoming obedient to death-- even death on a cross"* (Philippians 2:8).

Chapter 5: Breaking the Yoke of Poverty

> *"Christ has redeemed us from the curse of the law, having become a curse for us, for it is written, and "Cursed is everyone who hangs on a tree" (Galatians 3:13).*

These verses help us to understand and confirm that we are not under the curse of poverty. Jesus has paid the price. Not only are we free from the curse of poverty, but God's plan for us is also to prosper:

> *"And you shall remember the Lord your God, for it is He who gives you power to get wealth, that He may establish His covenant which He swore to your fathers, as it is this day"(Deuteronomy 8:18).*

In this verse, God calls us into remembrance about wealth. He says "think about it. I can empower and enable you to make wealth, I did it in the past, and I will do it again; my reason for doing this is linked to the covenant I swore to your fathers.'

This verse makes it clear that the reason why God will give you the power to get wealth is that He wants to establish a covenant that he swore to your fathers. The reason why we Africans, in particular, find it difficult to build wealth is that some of our parents did not have any covenant with God, but rather they did with idolatry.

However, every born again Christian is a child of God, and as such we have an understanding of the power of God and access to it. John 1: 12,

"But as many as received Him, to them He gave the right to become children of God, to those who believe in His name."

The western world though knowing God less now seem to make money more and more because past generations understood the principles behind the covenant of prosperity or wealth making.

The critical points in Deuteronomy 8:18 are:

- To remember the Lord; and
- Fathers

Without these two points, the sentence (passage) doesn't make sense. The fathers refer to Abraham, Isaac, and Jacob. The fourth dispensation of the promise is the believers. In Isaiah 51:2, it, *"Look unto Abraham, your father, and unto Sarah that bare you: for I called him alone, and blessed him, and increased him."*

This scripture is a recipe for our financial breakthrough. It tells us to think of what our father Abraham did and what our mother Sarah did. The scripture says dig into their lives, for I (God) called him (Abraham). I (God) called him alone. And then I blessed him! And then I increased him! Thus, if we as Christians can hear God's calling and look into the life of Abraham, searching for that which blessed Abraham and that which increased him, then by so doing, we will be blessed.

Chapter 5: Breaking the Yoke of Poverty

What did Abraham do? I mentioned these in a previous chapter)

Abraham refused the spoils of war (ill-gotten wealth); for he had met with the Pure Source which never runs dry and had entered into a covenant of wealth with the Source (Gen 14:18-24)

In remembering this, the verse calls us to remember our fathers. It is clear that we cannot build wealth unless we remember the fathers. If we take away everything and just "remember the fathers," we will be on the right track.

HOW TO REMEMBER THE FATHERS

In this context Abraham, Isaac and Jacob's father is God, and that is where the revelation of remembrance comes from. We must remember, our God at the starting point of our journey towards financial triumph and all throughout our days.

1. ACKNOWLEDGE GOD

Dec 18:8 makes it clear that God's role in the process of making wealth cannot be quantified, and God wants us to remember that fact. Abraham, Isaac, and Jacob, lived their lives guided by this principle.

2. KEEPING HIS WORD

When you keep God's word and base everything on His word, you will experience wealth, Abraham, Isaac, and Jacob did this. And by so doing, God gave them divine ideas on which they anchored their strategy for wealth on; God will do the same for you! Often it could be through a trade that you have worked hard on. For example, Abraham had a trade, and he understood inside out how that trade worked and worked out his God's giving strategy through that.

See Gen 30:32; Jacob was also given a technique for wealth making because he remembered and relied on God.

> "Let me pass through all your flock today, removing from there all the speckled and spotted sheep, and all the brown ones among the lambs, and the spotted and speckled among the goats; and these shall be my wages."

Sometimes it can be a gift – Joseph used his gift or gifts to his advantage.

If you have a brilliant idea suddenly, know its God that put it into you and follow it through. God will also give you a word to back up that idea. Your ability to remember that word continuously and to hold on to it is part of remembering that it is God who gives the ability to make wealth.

Chapter 5: Breaking the Yoke of Poverty

3. ANCHOR HIS WORD TO YOUR PROJECT OR YOUR CHALLENGE

It is important that as Christians, we must in addition to always relying on the word; anchor His word to our project or whatever challenges we face.

When I was going through the problem of completing an estate project that I had started, God gave me a word in Zechariah 4:9

> *"It says the hands of Zerubbabel have laid the foundation of this temple, his hands must finish it. I stood on this word, knowing that God who has spoken cannot fail."*

Another word which God gave to me is 1 Samuel 7:12

> *"Then Samuel took a stone and set it up between Mizpah and Shen, and called its name Ebenezer, [c]saying, "Thus far the Lord has helped us." "*

As His children, God speaks to us. It is our responsibility to hear the word and run with it.

If God is the architect of a project, your business, your career, your ministry, He will always give you a word or speak to you. You must be able to hear. You will hear many voices from the enemy, but your antenna must be tuned to hear God. And you can then stand on that word.

4. THROUGH THE SHARING OF TESTIMONIES

Another act of remembrance comes through the sharing of testimonies: Deuteronomy 8:2.

> *"And you shall remember that the Lord your God led you all the way these forty years in the wilderness, to humble you and test you, to know what was in your heart, whether you would keep His commandments or not."*

When you keep His commandments, and He blesses you, you must share your testimony, and it must be shared in humility, giving all the praise and glory to God and ensuring that it encourages the hearer to have an "increase in their faith level."

5. ACKNOWLEDGING GOD AS THE ONLY SOURCE

Remembrance is also demonstrated through acknowledging God as the Only Source.

Deuteronomy 8:3 tells us that

> *"But man lives by every word that proceeds out of the mouth... Some prayers will never be answered if God knows that man would not share His testimonies".*

Doing that, you are remembering God.

> *And you shall remember that the Lord your God led you all the way these forty years in the wilderness, to humble you and test you, to know what was in your heart, whether you would keep His commandments or not. So He humbled you, allowed you to hunger, and*

Chapter 5: Breaking the Yoke of Poverty

> *fed you with manna which you did not know nor did your fathers know, that He might make you know that man shall not live by bread alone; but man lives by every word that proceeds from the mouth of the Lord. Your garments did not wear out on you, nor did your foot swell these forty years. You should know in your heart that as a man chastens his son, so the Lord your God chastens you. "Therefore you shall keep the commandments of the Lord your God, to walk in His ways and to fear Him. For the Lord your God is bringing you into a good land, a land of brooks of water, of fountains and springs, that flow out of valleys and hills; a land of wheat and barley, of vines and fig trees and pomegranates, a land of olive oil and honey; a land in which you will eat bread without scarcity, in which you will lack nothing; a land whose stones are iron and out of whose hills you can dig copper. When you have eaten and are full, then you shall bless the Lord your God for the good land which He has given you.*

6. HAVING A HEART OF GRATITUDE

Deuteronomy 8:10 says to us:

> *"When you have eaten and are full, then you shall bless the Lord your God for the good land which He has given you."*

Gratitude is not limited to just saying thank you. The dictionary describes gratitude as "the quality of being thankful; readiness to show appreciation for and to return kindness. So as Christians, how do you demonstrate this in practice?

Let's take a look at Galatians 6:7-10 to help us with this:

> "Let him who is taught the word share in all good things with him who teaches. (You can bless teachers and pastors that teach you the word). Do not be deceived, God is not mocked; for whatever a man sows, that he will also reap. (You can sow a seed). For he who sows to his flesh will of the flesh reap corruption, but he who sows to the Spirit will of the Spirit reap everlasting life. (You can sow to eternal life by soul winning). And let us not grow weary while doing good, for in due season we shall reap if we do not lose heart. You can do good. Therefore, as we have opportunity, (you can give whenever you have the opportunity to) let us do good to all, (you can give to all people in and out of the church) especially to those who are of the household of faith. You can give to people in need in the church."

God wants us to be custodians of His wealth. He reminds us in this verse that He has a covenant with our lineage which is linked to our being prosperous. We can also see this in 3 John 1:2. John wrote to Gaius the beloved "that you may prosper," it could have stopped there if God's intention was to limit this to money, it is not prospering in money alone but in everything that pertains to living an exemplary life and an abundance life – John10:10 God's desire is that we live well and live long just as he promised Abraham and manifested it in Genesis 24:1. He blessed him in everything. It extends the blessing to, "good health as your soul prospers."

Chapter 6

Access to Financial Triumph through His Covenant

God in His infinite mercies blesses us with prosperity. It is an advantage that enables you to be far ahead of every other person. Prosperity is not a promise, being wealthy is not a promise; it goes beyond a promise to a covenant. Every promise comes with a condition, once the condition is fulfilled, that promise becomes a covenant. As seen in Psalm 89:36, a promise can be broken, but a covenant cannot be broken, 'His seed shall endure forever, and his throne as the sun before me. This is a covenant.'

Let us consider how this might work. Exodus 23:25 says,

> "But you shall serve the LORD your God, and He will bless your bread and your water; and I will remove sickness from your midst. There shall be no one miscarrying or barren in your land; I will fulfil the number of your days.

A believer can hold on to this as a promise from God; however, that promise can get broken because of Malachi 3:8-9,'

> 'Will a man rob God? Yet ye have robbed me. But ye say, wherein have we robbed thee? In tithes and offerings. Ye are cursed with a curse: for ye have robbed me, even this whole nation.'

The flip side to this is the promise in Exodus 23:25 can move into covenant through the words in Malachi 3:10-11

> "Bring ye all the tithes into the storehouse, that there may be meat in mine house, and prove me now herewith, saith the Lord of hosts, if I will not open you the windows of heaven, and pour you out a blessing, that there shall not be room enough to receive it. And I will rebuke the devourer for your sakes, and he shall not destroy the fruits of your ground; neither shall your vine cast her fruit before the time in the field, saith the Lord of hosts."

The Apostle John in 3 John 1:2 said,

> "Beloved, I pray that you may prosper in all things and be in health, just as your soul prospers."

This covers three areas regarding God's plan concerning His children which makes it plain that God's plan for us is not limited to financial prosperity but also prosperity in health, body, and soul.

Chapter 6: Access to Financial Triumph through His Covenant

So why is there a gap between most believers and financial triumph and how does God release us from the yoke of poverty?

To answer these questions, we must understand that beyond our salvation, we are to spend the rest of our lives 'partnering' with God to bring into reality His promises and covenants for our lives. We need to understand that there is a "partnering" relationship required between God and man in actualising financial triumph; above that of being born again. That partnership relationship is birth at the point where we come to understand that prosperity is part of God's promises and activated by covenant.

THE THREE KEY COVENANTS

1. The covenant of obedience
2. The covenant of sacrificial giving
3. The covenant of wisdom.

1. THE COVENANT OF OBEDIENCE

To help understand the covenant of obedience, let us look at Exodus 19:5 which says

> *"Now therefore, if you will indeed obey My voice and keep My covenant, then you shall be a special treasure to Me above all people."*

We note in this verse the word "if." This is the key word in this covenant agreement. The people of Israel responded by saying they were willing to do all that God commanded them. The agreement was ratified by blood. See Exodus 24:4-8.

> "And Moses wrote all the words of the Lord. And he rose early in the morning, and built an altar at the foot of the mountain, and twelve pillars according to the twelve tribes of Israel. Then he sent young men of the children of Israel, who offered burnt offerings and sacrificed peace offerings of oxen to the Lord. And Moses took half the blood and put it in basins, and half the blood he sprinkled on the altar. Then he took the Book of the Covenant and read in the hearing of the people. And they said, "All that the Lord has said we will do, and be obedient." And Moses took the blood, sprinkled it on the people, and said, "This is the blood of the covenant which the Lord has made with you according to all these words."

Also in Proverbs 3: 1-6:

> "My son, do not forget my teaching, but keep my commands in your heart, for they will prolong your life many years and bring you peace and prosperity. Let love and faithfulness never leave you; bind them around your neck, write them on the tablet of your heart. Then you will win favour and a good name in the sight of God and man." Trust in the Lord with all your heart, and lean not on your own understanding; in all your ways acknowledge Him, and He shall direct[a] your paths.

The above passages show that in obeying God's commandments, we will experience length of days, long

Chapter 6: Access to Financial Triumph through His Covenant

life, and peace. An obedient heart to the things of God is assured of complete financial triumph.

Jesus Himself is an example of the covenant of obedience. We read in Philippians 2:8-9, how through His obedience, we now enjoy freedom and victory:

> *"He humbled himself, becoming obedient unto death, even to the death of the cross. For which cause, God also hath exalted him and hath given him a name which is above all names: that in the name of Jesus every knee should bow, of those that are in heaven, on earth, and under the earth: and that every tongue should confess that the Lord Jesus Christ is in the glory of God the Father."*

Ultimately, if Christ chose not to obey God, there would not have been salvation for anyone.

Notice Matthew 6:33 as well which states

> *"But seek first his kingdom and his righteousness, and all these things will be given to you as well. God is clearly saying to us that there is a condition through which everything gets added to us, and that condition is linked to seeking His Kingdom and seeking His righteousness."*

Joshua came into triumph through the law of obedience see Joshua 1:8. It would have been impossible for Joshua to lead the children of Israel into the promise land had he failed to listen to God.

2. THE COVENANT OF SACRIFICIAL GIVING

Sacrificial giving is the essence of our salvation. God moved with love, gave His one and only begotten Son so that we may not die but have eternal life (John 3:16). We quote this verse so often that we fail to recognise the depth and the essence of this sacrifice. God Himself gave a clear example of this and showed us that freedom is achieved through the act of sacrificial giving.

We can relate to the fact that for every promise of scripture, there are conditions to be met. For example, it takes faith to receive healing from God; it takes faith to receive the good news of salvation even though the price has been paid. As stated above when conditions attached to a promise are fulfilled, we enter into a covenant relationship with God.

It is the same with financial triumph. We read the story of Abraham, Jacob, and Isaac and we quote these scriptures quite a lot; but to enjoy the blessings of Abraham in whom God blessed with all things, we have to do what Abraham did to receive this blessing from the Lord. Abraham worked by faith; He had absolute faith in God and His word. Abraham's attitude was, "if God said it, then that settles it." The Word of God was final to him. The same must be for us.

God's will is for us to have financial triumph. The enemy's will for us is to live a life of struggle and misery.

Chapter 6: Access to Financial Triumph through His Covenant

Let's now consider a few people in the Bible who had the understanding of how to combine the law of obedience with the law of sacrificial giving to trigger covenant of financial breakthrough.

In Genesis 8:22, as God was speaking to Noah, He said,

> *"As long as the earth endures, seedtime and harvest, cold and heat, summer and winter, day and night will never cease."*

Prior to God speaking this verse, Noah had offered a sacrifice to the Lord which was pleasing to Him. God was, therefore, pleased to establish His covenant in return for Noah's act of obedience and sacrificial giving. If we continue to Genesis 9:1, we see the fulfilment of this which came to pass through a partnering and covenant relationship between Noah and God. *"Then God blessed Noah and his sons, saying to them, "Be fruitful and increase in number and fill the earth."*

Let us also consider King Solomon, who, after literally sacrificing a thousand burnt offerings, the Lord appeared to him by night and said,

> *"I have heard your prayer and have chosen this place for myself as a house of sacrifice!" (2 Chronicles 7:12).*

By Solomon's act of obedience and sacrificial giving, God proceeded to establish a covenant with Solomon from verse 13 onwards.

""When I shut up the heavens so that there is no rain, or command locusts to devour the land or send a plague among my people, 14 if my people, who are called by my name, will humble themselves and pray and seek my face and turn from their wicked ways, then will I hear from heaven and will forgive their sin and will heal their land. 15 Now my eyes will be open and my ears attentive to the prayers offered in this place. 16 I have chosen and consecrated this temple so that my Name may be there forever. My eyes and my heart will always be there."

In Acts 10:4, we see Cornelius, having a similar encounter as a result of his giving:

"About the ninth hour of the day he clearly saw in a vision an angel of God who had just come in and said to him, "Cornelius!" 4 And fixing his gaze on him and being much alarmed, he said, "What is it, Lord?" And he said to him, "Your prayers and alms have ascended as a memorial before God. "

The above examples confirm the power of sacrificial giving; the assurance of financial triumph and that prosperity is not just a promise but a covenant. Perhaps at this point, we need to be clear about the difference between a covenant and a promise.

The dictionary defines promise as 'a declaration that something will or will not be done, given by ones express assurance on which expectation is to be based. It is something that has the effect of an express assurance; and an indication of what may be expected.'

Chapter 6: Access to Financial Triumph through His Covenant

Covenant, on the other hand, is 'an agreement, usually formal, between two or more persons to do or not do something specified; Covenant is always linked to an incidental clause or an agreement. Covenant is activated by a fulfilled promise as explained earlier.'

That is, a promise is usually one sided whereas a covenant is premised on one of the parties being superior assuring the other party that on fulfilling a promise/condition, some form of benefit will be triggered.

Furthermore, a covenant is a conditional or operational promise. Deuteronomy 8:18 and Genesis 8:20-22 are good examples of covenants.

We also know that where individuals in the Old or the New Testament stand on God's Word and walk in the covenant by sacrifice, God always gives financial triumph.

Other relevant verses on Covenant

Isaiah 30:1, Joshua 1:8, Deuteronomy 8:18, Genesis 17:1-2, Job 36:11and Psalms 25:12 are excellent examples of making a covenant with God.

Let's look at 2 Corinthians 9:6-10.

> "Whoever sows sparingly will also reap sparingly, and whoever sows generously will also reap generously. Each of you should give what you have decided in your heart to give, not reluctantly or under compulsion, for God loves a cheerful giver.8And God

is able to bless you abundantly, so that in all things at all times, having all that you need, you will abound in every good work.9As it is written: "They have freely scattered their gifts to the poor; their righteousness endures forever 10Now He who supplies seed to the sewer and bread for food will also supply and increase your store of seed and will enlarge the harvest of your righteousness."

The above affirms that giving is one of God's main ways of releasing us from the yoke of poverty. Giving is an anchor of prosperity.

In Psalm 50:5, God calls for a calling and a gathering of his saints together to Him for blessings.

"Gather My saints together to Me, Those who have made a covenant with Me by sacrifice."

Covenant giving is a way of divine giving to the Lord. We have heard of pastors in top ministries who have declared that they can never be poor based on the assurance they have through Covenant giving. I know for sure that I can never be poor because I have entered into a covenant of giving with God by sacrifice, and God honours His Words. It is not a boast; it is an assurance of the faithfulness of God. Someone said being poor is a state of mind. I agree. You may be asset rich and cash broke, you are still potentially rich, but as a child of God, you should not be poor.

As believers, we all have heavenly accounts. Every seed that we sow will go into this account to harvest when needed. It is governed by the requirement of action from both sides by agreement and an automatic triggering of results, regardless of the circumstance. This is the reason why it is possible for an unbeliever to trigger the promises of prosperity and riches by operating by the principles of covenant prosperity – it is purely a law of nature for which, if the conditions are meant, the desired result will be produced.

Here we are discussing Christian giving. It says give and it shall be given unto you, good measure, pressed down, shaking together, running over (Luke 6:38).

God is looking for wealth custodians; Christians that will walk with Him based on His covenant and His principles. He does not want us to wait until we are wealthy before we give sacrificially to Him. God takes us into a place of sacrifice beyond what we can give. For this last point see 2 Corinthians 8:3-5;

> "For I bear witness that according to their ability, yes, and beyond their ability, they were freely willing, 4imploring us with much urgency that we would receive the gift and the fellowship of the ministering to the saints. And not only as we had hoped, but they first gave themselves to the Lord, and then to us by the will of God."

3. THE COVENANT OF THE LAW OF WISDOM

The law of wisdom is important and you can find the law of wisdom in two usages in the book of Proverbs:

Proverbs 3:1-2

> *"My son, do not forget my law but let your heart keep my commands, for length of days and long life, and peace they will add to you."*

The above passage assures us of two things (long life and peace).

In Proverbs 3:3,

> *"Let not mercy and truth forsake you, bind them around your neck, write them on the tablets of your heart."*
>
> *Verse 4 - "and so find favour and high esteem in the sight of God and man."*
>
> *Verse 5 - "trust in the Lord with all your heart and lean not on your own understandings in all ways acknowledge him and he shall direct your path."*

Do not forget from the first one. He says, learn to keep His commandments.

> *Verse 7 - "do not be wise in your own eye, fear the Lord and depart from evil, it will be health to your flesh and strength to your bones."*

Now this is where I am going, and it says 'honour the Lord with your possessions and with your first fruits with the first fruit of all your increase. When you have done the above, i.e. you keep my law, you honour the Lord, and then your barns will be filled with plenty and your vat overflow with new wine. My sons do not despise the law

Chapter 6: Access to Financial Triumph through His Covenant

of the Lord nor detest his correction. Verse 12, for whom the Lord loves, He corrects just as a father, the son in whom he delights. Verse 13 happy is the man who finds wisdom (that I say is a law of wisdom) and the man who gains understanding.

Verse 15, she is more precious than rubies and all the things you may desire cannot compare with her, if you find her that true law of wisdom, rubies will be nothing to you, and everything that you desire now will not be compared with wisdom.

Verses 16, length of days in her right hand, in her left hand are riches and honour.

Verse 17, she is a tree of life to those who take hold of her and happy are all who retain her.

I say, today, as you seek and find the law of wisdom you will retain her and hold unto her, your vat shall continuously be overflowing. Amen.

Long life will be your portion, blessings will be your portion, and curses will not be able to come near you in the mighty name of Jesus. Amen.

In Proverbs 4:1, we read

> *"'Hear my children, the instructions of your father and give attention to know understanding,' for I give you good doctrine, do not forsake my law (the law of wisdom), keep my commands and live, get wisdom, get understanding."*

Not only can you keep wisdom, but you can also get wisdom.

It goes on,

> "Do not forget nor turn away from the words of my mouth."
>
> Verse 6 - "do not forsake her and she will preserve you, and she will keep you."
>
> Verse 7 - "wisdom is the principal thing, therefore get wisdom, and in all your getting, get understanding."

If you go further, it says,

> "If you exalt her, she will promote you; she will embrace you as you embrace her."

As you go on the verses, it begins to tell you the beauty of wisdom, the ornament of grace, the crown of glory and how it will deliver you.

As you get wisdom you get money, you get prosperity, and you get blessings, unexplained blessings, overflowing blessings and supernatural wealth in the mighty name of Jesus. That is the law of wisdom.

These three covenants are pulled together by trusting God and the law of giving. If you consider at Psalm 20:1-6; it gives the assurance of what we have in trusting and giving to God.

The psalmist renders a resounding assured, confident declaration in God which every Christian must have. He

Chapter 6: Access to Financial Triumph through His Covenant

links this to the giving of offering and the acceptance of sacrifice.

He says:

- God will answer you in the day of trouble,
- His name will defend you; it says "may He send you help "not only will you be answered but you will also be defended.
- He will send us help from the sanctuary and strength out of Zion.
- He will remember all your offerings and accept our sacrifice. He who gives in offering and sacrifices is bound to be helped in times of trouble; he is obliged to be answered, and he is bound to receive help from the Lord.
- He will grant us according to our heart's desire.
- We will rejoice in our salvation.
- In the name of our Lord Jesus, we will set up our banner.
- May the Lord fulfil all our petitions, not just some petitions, but all our petitions. Amen.

Now I know that the Lord saves His anointed, He will answer him from His holy heaven with His saving strength of His right hand.

So God brings you help, God remembers your offerings, every time you stretch out your hand to God he gives you divine protection.

Giving not only brings everything good, but it also provides you with good health, but it also rids you of parasites, it takes the devourer out of your life, He blesses you beyond your imagination, and it moves you closer to God.

In the book of Genesis 17:1, God said to Abraham *"walk before Me and be blameless."* What God is saying is *"walk before me and have my nature."* It is God's nature to give.

One of the chief catalysts for Abraham's incredible wealth was giving, and you can have that too.

As you read this book, you can break every curse of poverty, standing on Isaiah 10:27. Decree that this yoke is broken. It says that his burden will be lifted away from your shoulder, and His yoke from your neck and the yoke will be destroyed because of the anointing oil. Just say it and believe. Amen.

Under the new covenant by the price paid by Jesus, we have the Holy Spirit that represents this experience of the anointing oil. We know how important this is, as it is the anointing that breaks and destroys the yoke (Isaiah 10:27). The yoke of poverty is broken over you in Jesus Name. Amen.

Chapter 6: Access to Financial Triumph through His Covenant

Firstly, I need to say that you do not need anointing oil, water, handkerchief et cetera for power. What you need is faith in the Word and its authority. However, there are occasions where some people believe in the extra efficacy of instruments like the anointing oil, handkerchief, water, candles/incense. And there are scriptures to support these (for example, regarding the use of anointing oil, please see Isaiah 10:27, James 5:14 and Mark 16:13; and for the use of handkerchiefs, please see Acts 19:12).

With the above in mind, please visit the prayers at the end of this book. It is at your discretion whether you anoint yourself, please do what you are comfortable with.

What is important is living a righteous life and believing in the power of God to transform and heal. If you believe in the power that comes through the Word and agree with me by faith on those set of prayers, every burden of poverty is taken from your shoulder, and every yoke is destroyed in Jesus' name, Amen!

We will round up this chapter by restating seven principles that govern sacrificial giving: These are:

1. It secures God's commitment to blessing you (Genesis 22:16-18).

2. It establishes a partnership relationship between you and God (Genesis 17:1-8).

3. You have at your disposal a divine weapon and tool to confuse the enemy, each time you give a

sacrificial offering; the devil is confused, jealous and unsettled. It happened in the case of Cain and Abel (Genesis 4:1-5).

4. It secures a continuity of blessing – see Isaac in (Genesis 26:12-14).

5. It brings about long life, health, and prosperity (3 John1:2).

6. Sacrificial giving brings you into being a custodian of God's wealth (Deuteronomy 8:18).

7. Sacrificial giving allows for speed in accomplishment (1 King 3: 4-14).

Chapter 7

Access to Spiritual Speed

In this chapter we will learn about how to tap into the anointing of speed for attaining financial breakthrough. We will also learn how to:

- Turn up the supernatural for the purpose of financial breakthrough;
- Have the edge in the race; and
- Stay ahead of others and why that is important.

Ultimately, we will learn how to work towards understanding how to rely on God and His principles to come into His plans for us to be prosperous. Before going further, take the time to familiarise yourself with the story of how the children of Israel began to conquer the Promised Land of Canaan in Deuteronomy 2.

One of the things we have to learn as Christians is how to take advantage of the privileges we have in Christ, to use God's principles to activate divine speed in order to be triumphant in financial things.

CONFIDENCE

1 John 5:14-15, introduces us to the first principle of how this can be achieved - the activation of the supernatural through confidence in God.

> "Now this is the confidence that we have in Him, that if we ask anything according to His will, He hears us. And if we know that He hears us, whatever we ask, we know that we have the petitions that we have asked of Him."

What is confidence?

The English dictionary defines it as "the feeling or belief that one can have faith in or rely on someone or something."

You cannot sell a product if you do not believe in it. It is confidence that helps you to press on even in the face of challenges. We understand from this passage the need to have confidence in God, the need to know that He is above all, He owns all and He is in all. We understand the need to ask and to ask according to His will, knowing and believing that because we have asked in His will, the result is certain. He will answer! The word of God advises us clearly to "have confidence" as the first and core principle.

BOLDNESS

Once we have confidence, we can progress to the next principle, the principle of boldness. This we find in Matthew 11:12. This scripture says,

> *"From the days of John the Baptist until now, the kingdom of heaven has been subjected to violence, and violent people have been raiding it."*

This scripture makes it clear that the things of God and the things of the triumphant are not served on a platter of gold. They are not things that we stumble into or casually walk into. The things of God are things claimed with boldness, with violence and by force. Having boldness must be combined with having confidence

What is boldness?

The dictionary meaning of boldness means "not hesitating or fearful in the face of actual or possible danger or rebuff; courageous and daring." As Christians, we must not be timid.

PROGRESS

The third principle is understanding the need to move and understand that God is at the centre of that move. See Deuteronomy 2:1-2.

> *"Then we turned and journeyed into the wilderness of the Way of the Red Sea, as the Lord spoke to me, and we skirted Mount Seir for many days. And the Lord*

spoke to me, saying: 'You have skirted this mountain long enough; turn northward.'"

We see in this verse that the children of Israel may have had confidence in God, may have shown boldness in taking the things of God to get to this point, but at some point, they became complacent because they started enjoying the cosiness of the environment. They became contented at a place of low achievement. Then God said to them, you have skirted around this mountain for too long, enough of the skirting, it is now time to turn. The word "skirt" is quite significant; it can be likened to a lady's skirt, and God's intervention here can be likened to the effect of a strong wind on the skirt. The picture the Lord gave me here is the wind being the Holy Spirit. When the wind blows, it blows the skirt in any direction it chooses, and the direction is determined by the wind, not the person. God is saying to us in this verse, stop skirting around, you have stayed in that spot for too long, make a move and turn north into the city which God has planned. A northward turn will move and bring us near to the land of promise and fulfilment.

God wants a destiny-changing experience for us, once we have confidence, once we have boldness, once we realise the need to move, God backs us up with a destiny-changing experience. We see this in Deuteronomy 2:24. He says to us that He has given us possession of the land,

Chapter 7: Access to Spiritual Speed

> *"'Rise, take your journey, and cross over the River Arnon. Look, I have given into your hand Sihon the Amorite, king of Heshbon, and his land. Begin to possess it, and engage him in battle."*

As He did with the children of Israel, God expects us to meet the following key responsibilities:

1. TO RISE

Take our journey (we each have an individual journey that is specifically tailored by God for us). Be responsible for your assignment.

2. CROSSOVER

In crossing over, there is an action and a requirement of taking a bold step, moving from one position into another.

3. TO LOOK

Once we have done these, God requires from us a strengthening of our vision and sight. He says '"look, see that I have given it into your hands."' The 'look' here is different from just looking; it extends to "seeing." This type of "seeing" refers to looking beyond the physical, and deep into the future. Examples of this can be found in Zechariah 4:1, where the prophet Zechariah was asked by an angel of God to 'see,'

> "Now the angel who talked with me came back and wakened me, as a man who is wakened out of his sleep. And he said to me, 'What do you see?'"

Again, the prophet Jeremiah was asked a similar question in Jeremiah 1:11,

> "The word of the LORD came to me: 'What do you see, Jeremiah?' 'I see the branch of an almond tree,' I replied."

Both Zechariah and Jeremiah 'saw' by the Holy Spirit. That is the same 'sight' we need to have to increase our progress in becoming financially triumphant.

4. TO POSSESS

God gave the children of Israel an assurance of total victory over the land of Canaan. Today, His assurance of victory to us concerns various spiritual blessings which include financial triumph. However, He wants us to know that, as with the Israelites, there will be a battle (or war, depending on the level of bondage et cetera) with the enemy before victory can be achieved. Each one of us has to be determined to take that which has been given to us. Every land of promise and victory is a higher level than the one on which we currently find ourselves, and with it comes its own giants. It is a different level of operation which we are being called into, and as such, to experience financial triumph, we must be prepared and ready to engage the enemy in battle. In confessing this verse, you

Chapter 7: Access to Spiritual Speed

can first, physically arise, secondly, see a picture the specific journey you wish to take, thirdly, take a crossover step - a bold action and fourthly, again, visualise the vision which God has given you.

Right now, that vision may seem an impossible dream because of the obstacles in the way but do not be discouraged. The Israelites were discouraged and never fulfilled their vision.

In 1 Samuel 30:8 David demonstrated this in practical terms. David inquired of the Lord; He had confidence that God hears (1 John 5:14-15), so he asked "Shall I pursue this raiding party? Will I overtake them?"

God's response was one of a call to boldness, just as we have described in Matthew 11:12 *("From the days of John the Baptist until now, the kingdom of heaven has been subjected to violence, and violent people have been raiding it")*.

God told David to pursue them. God is also telling you to take action and to be violently determined about your wish because not only will there be an overtaking; there will be a restoration of all.

God gave David not just a command backed by an assurance "pursuing and overtaking; He also provided an assurance of recovering all. Moreover, as David activated these commands, he experienced victory. The battle is never ours as stated in 2 Chronicles 20:17:

> *"You will not need to fight in this battle. Position yourselves, stand still and see the salvation of the Lord, who is with you, O Judah and Jerusalem!' Do not fear or be dismayed; tomorrow go out against them, for the Lord is with you."*

5. TAKE CONTROL

We are required to take control of the land. Without this, we cannot possess the land. The enemy must be fought, and we need to tie down the strong man. He is already a defeated foe as set out in Colossians 2:15-17:

> *"Having disarmed principalities and powers, He made a public spectacle of them, triumphing over them in it. So let no one judge you in food or in drink, or regarding a festival or a new moon or Sabbaths, which are a shadow of things to come, but the substance is of Christ."*

Do not be discouraged because where the Lord is taking us is a land of milk and honey; there will be giants (bigger competitors, commercial rivals, and determined usurpers) in that land. In every land of victory, there are giants already occupying it. In this season as we go on to possess, there will, as a matter of course, be resistance.

There is a higher devil for the higher level God is taking you into. In fulfilling any purpose, there are giants. That is why we need confidence and boldness in God to take hold of the land.

Chapter 7: Access to Spiritual Speed

Taking hold of the land is action led, there needs to be an arising, taking over, and crossing over and then God will give you the land. Let us see Luke 16:16,

> *"The law and the prophets were until John. Since that time the kingdom of God has been preached, and everyone is pressing into it."*

This verse is very similar to Matthew 11:12. It is action led, and it calls for a pressing. The Kingdom of God and entering into purpose and financial triumph is not a cruise or a gliding affair. It is a marathon race that requires strength and pressing ahead.

The key steps we have learned so far are as follows:

- We have to have the confidence in Christ (1 John 5:14-15)
- We have to be bold (Matthew 11:12)
- We have to possess the land, recognise that there will be giants and enemies and be prepared through God's might, to challenge these (Deuteronomy 2:2)
- We have to understand the steps towards our God-given destiny and His design for us (Deuteronomy 2:2, 24)
- Know that if you are not willing to be discomforted, you cannot be comfortable.
- We have to press forward (Luke 16:16)

SOME PRACTICAL EXAMPLES

Example 1: Daniel 3:12-19

Here we read about the three Hebrew boys; Shadrach, Meshach, and Abednego. This text provides an excellent illustration of how the principles of divine speed work.

The three Hebrew boys had been taken as slaves from Israel to Babylon. They refused to bow down and worship the foreign king. They were sent to burn in the fiery furnace.

There was a divine intervention by God in what could have been the end of the three young Israelites. We know the background of this story in the sense that these three young men chose to stand their ground in the things of God.

They activated the five principles of divine speed.

1. CONFIDENCE (1 John 5:14-15)

The three Hebrew boys spoke with confidence about their God; they had an assurance that God will fight on their behalf and equally were ready for the consequence if a physical manifestation of victory did not take place.

> *"Shadrach, Meshach, and Abednego answered and said to the king, "O Nebuchadnezzar, we have no need to answer you in this matter"(Daniel 3:16).*

2. BOLDNESS BEFORE THE KING (Matthew 11:12)

"If that is the case, our God whom we serve is able to deliver us from the burning fiery furnace, and He will deliver us from your hand, O king. But if not, let it be known to you, O king, that we do not serve your gods, nor will we worship the gold image which you have set up" (Daniel 3:17).

3. THEY PRESSED FORWARD AND WERE WILLING TO BE THROWN INTO THE FUNNEL OF FIRE (Luke 16:16)

"And he commanded certain mighty men of valour who were in his army to bind Shadrach, Meshach, and Abednego, and cast them into the burning fiery furnace. Then these men were bound in their coats, their trousers, their turbans, and their other garments, and were cast into the midst of the burning fiery furnace. Therefore, because the king's command was urgent, and the furnace exceedingly hot, the flame of the fire killed those men who took up Shadrach, Meshach, and Abednego. And these three men, Shadrach, Meshach, and Abednego, fell down bound into the midst of the burning fiery furnace" (Daniel 3:20-23).

Needing to possess a miracle or activate speedy divine and supernatural intervention clearly involves tackling giants, as can be seen with the young men, there was a challenge which they needed to overcome. Because of their actions, from verse twenty-six, onwards, the King came to acknowledge their God as the High God. He not only recognised Him as God but the High God, greater that his gods.

The story reveals to us that if we believe in God, God will expedite a speedy intervention that will lead to our victory. For these three young Jews, they stood on the principles of integrity. They were willing to leave their comfort zone, ready to do the battle and willing to put their trust in God.

We need to realise that no one comes into a place of victory without having won a battle with the enemy. The assurance that God gives us is one of victory.

Example 2: Daniel 6:10

Similar to the experience of the three young Jews, Daniel was asked to compromise on his position about serving and worshiping God.

Just as with the three young Jews, Daniel stood his ground, he demonstrated confidence in the Word of God and boldness in his faith in God, he pressed forward despite experiencing discomfort, he overtook and overcame in the battle, and again the name of God was glorified.

Example 3: Luke 19:1

Zacchaeus made a decision to achieve his life's purpose. He was determined in making an effort to see Jesus. He realised that his weakness was his height. There

Chapter 7: Access to Spiritual Speed

was a crowd, and because of his height, it would be impossible for him to see Jesus.

For Zacchaeus, seeing Jesus was his ultimate aim, he realised his stature might prevent him, so he made every effort not to focus on his weakness but to rely on his strengths. He ran ahead, climbed a tree and got to see Jesus as He passed by that tree. That act gave him victory. By applying the rules of skills development and adding this to the skills of operating in the supernatural, he was able to gain victory.

Zacchaeus weakness was subordinate to his strengths. He made a decision not to let his lack of height stop him. He had three areas of strengths and one weakness. He did not focus on his weakness but rather on his strengths.

Think about yourself and your strengths. If you were in Zacchaeus' position would you have thrown a pity party about your weaknesses or would you have acted in your strengths? As individuals, if we were in the same situation with Zacchaeus, would we look inwards, identify our skills and use this to navigate ourselves to where God wants us to be? If Zacchaeus did not exercise his strength, forget about his weakness, and focus on using his strength, he would not have gained victory.

In Luke 19:5 Jesus was interested in Zacchaeus actions; He called him to his presence. Jesus asked him to come down because he was going to stay in his house that night. This is a typical example of how divine speed works in the life of a believer who chooses to practice God's will.

Zacchaeus could not see Jesus but knew the way that Jesus would take. He aligned himself with this "way" and by so doing secured his victory and his destiny. A significant number of miracles that Jesus did, he did them by the wayside. Even where it seems like we cannot see Jesus, we must know His ways and work in His ways.

Example 4: John 5:1

We see an example of another man, who was in a situation where he needed help. In this example, this man did everything opposite to what Zacchaeus did. He was in the same position for 38 years. He made no effort to identify how he could break free. When Jesus met him in that position and asked him if he wanted to be free and made well, he gave a silly answer, "I have no man to help me." He was wallowing in self-pity. This individual had the gift of talking, yet he was not able or willing to use it to gain his victory. He could have used his strength - "talking." To talk himself to victory but he chose to focus on his weakness. He was waiting for someone to lift him up. He remained in a place of low esteem, with people with similar weaknesses. He did not make a move to seek a helper or to motivate himself. A lot of us are in this state where instead of focusing on our strengths and using our God giving strength for victory, we dwell on our weakness and try to justify why the situation is so bad.

Chapter 7: Access to Spiritual Speed

Having such an attitude will not bring us to the point of divine speed, as we can see; this individual was in this position for 38 years. (See an exposition of this subject in my book: Make that move right now).

We can compare this man's lack of motivation to an act of active inspiration. In Mark 2:3, in this example the man had a similar weakness to that of the man in John 5. He was crippled, and he also had the same strength. He could talk, we know of this strength because even though it was not mentioned, we can deduce from the text that he had persuaded four men to carry him. Not only did they carry him, but they also delivered him to the rooftop, removed the roof, and they brought him down before or into the presence of Jesus. This man must have had persuasive skills. He was able to connect with his helpers and was able to convince his helpers of the need to help him. As Christians, we must be able to excite someone to a point where the person sees the need to help. This in itself will bring about our breakthrough. Jesus saw how this man had used his strength to get him to a point of destiny; He crowned his effort by bringing him into fulfilment (Mark 2:5). When Jesus saw their faith, he said to the paralytic *"son of man your sins are forgiven you."*

If we take the time to read the text we will be able to identify all the ingredients that bring about victory - An underlying confidence that is a requirement for victory is to have an encounter with Jesus, the boldness of taking the required action, and engagement with the giants in the land and finally victory.

In Mark 2: 9-10 the Bible recalls,

> "9 Which is easier, to say to the paralytic, 'Your sins are forgiven you,' or to say, 'Arise, take up your bed and walk'? 10 But that you may know that the Son of Man has power on earth to forgive sins."

He said to the paralytic, I say to you, arise, take up your bed, and go to your house.

This man gained and experienced God's divine-speed through the principles of confidence, boldness, preparing, taking possession and engaging the Giants; he used his God's given strength, moved away from his weakness and focused on his strength. This gained him victory. This man also realised the power and strength of knowing how to connect with the right people. He knew whom to call for help, and he knew who to focus on for deliverance.

Let's compare this man's example to the experience of the Greeks in John 12:20 -21;

> "20 Now there were certain Greeks among those who came up to worship at the feast. 21 Then they came to Philip, who was from Bethsaida of Galilee, and asked him, saying, "Sir, we wish to see Jesus."22 Philip came and told Andrew, and in turn Andrew and Philip told Jesus."

We see in this verse that the Greeks were knowledgeable and seemed to know all. They did ask to

Chapter 7: Access to Spiritual Speed

see Jesus. However, we are not told that this meeting happened. Why would this have been the case? The channels of connection the Greeks were relying on were far off. They had come to the feast, had come up to Philip, who could not help and then had to go to ask Andrew and then Andrew and Philip then told Jesus. We can deduce from this that even Philip needed help. He was unable to approach Jesus directly; he needed to rely on Andrew, and in combination, they had no strategy. No confidence, no boldness, there was no urgency, and as a result, the outcomes were clearly different.

We see another example in the Bible: Luke 18:36 onwards: This blind man clearly had a weakness, he was blind, but he also had strength, he could talk, and he could hear.

We read that:

And hearing a multitude passing by, he asked what it meant. (This shows that he inquired, he sought for his breakthrough). He obviously seems to have asked the right people because they told him what was happening: "Jesus of Nazareth was passing by."

In verse 38, we see an activation of strength:

"38 And he cried out, saying, "Jesus, Son of David, have mercy on me!"

In verse 39, we see the giants in the land:

> "39 Then those who went before warned him that he should be quiet;"

In this same verse, we see him taking possession and engaging with the Giants.

> "But he cried out all the more, "Son of David, have mercy on me!"

So Jesus stood still and commanded him to be brought to Him.

Jesus stood still at the cry and sound of "Son of David, have mercy upon me." This man knew the Son, and he knew the power in the name and the blood! He pleaded the blood. Son of God, have mercy! He gave Jesus no choice than to turn and ask what he wanted.

We see in same verse 40 that this blind man needed to come out! And when he had come near, God asked Him what he wanted, and he said:

> "Lord, that I may receive my sight."42 Then Jesus said to him, "Receive your sight; your faith has made you well."

Let's see the story of the wise men in Mathew2:1 -4. In this example, God had given divine speed; God provided this in the form of a star. The wise men followed the star for a bit and then got diverted. In verse 2, their diversion took them to the camp of the enemy; they decided to ask

Chapter 7: Access to Spiritual Speed

from Herod. The wise men not only lost focus but also connected to the wrong helper. In doing this, their actions caused them to delay. That aspect of prophecy may have gone unfulfilled but God in His mercies brought them to the point of refocusing and by looking towards the star once again they were back on track to reach Jesus and to fulfil their destinies.

Today, God is calling us to a place of His divine speed which we can activate through confidence in Him (1 John 5:14-15); boldness; and pressing on (Luke 16:16 and Matthew 11:12).

We need to move away from our comfort zone (Deuteronomy 2:2) and realise that the land we are being called to possess requires an engagement with giants because it is a destiny changing Place. Deuteronomy2:24.

WEALTHY WAYS

Chapter 8

How to Make and Sustain Wealth by Appreciation

A key ingredient for any person or business that seeks to enter into and wishes to sustain financial breakthrough is to learn the art and act of appreciation. This includes being grateful, being thankful and being able to appreciate the source of one's blessings

> "In everything give thanks; for this is the will of God in Christ Jesus for you" (1 Thessalonians 5:18).

We express gratefulness through gratitude. The English dictionary describes grateful as feeling or showing appreciation for something done or received; and defines "thankful," as awareness and appreciative of a benefit (i.e., an expression of gratitude)

In Luke 17:11-17, we read about the ten lepers that were healed, and we learnt that only one of the lepers came back to express gratitude and to give thanks. All the ten lepers wanted healing; all cried out to God, but only one came back to give thanks. We read that the thoughtfulness of this one man was recognised in heaven as he was able to attain completion (wholeness) in addition to healing by returning to give thanks.

The leper that returned put into action Deuteronomy 8:18: "And you shall remember." This means He was aware of God expectations of us to reflect and recall His mercies and goodness towards us. He was also conscious of the source of his healing.

Verse 15-16 reads

> *"This one returned with a loud voice, glorifying God, he fell on his knees giving thanks, and he was a Samaritan."*

Even Jesus was surprised and as such asked for the whereabouts of the other nine.

The lesson behind this story is that there is great gain in giving thanks. It moves the individual from completion into wholesomeness. God expects that we are not just in a place of glory, not just a person of glory, not just in a position of giving but also in a position of gratitude, giving praise and acknowledging that all He had done for you. Every time we return to give God thanks, God gives us His promotion. This one leper came back, he fell at Jesus' feet and thanked the Lord, and as such, his blessing was greater than the others.

Chapter 8: How to Make and Sustain Wealth by Appreciation

In 1 Samuel 1:28 Hannah returned Samuel to the Lord with thanksgiving. Also see 1 Samuel 2:1-2. Let's study the peculiarity of Hannah prayers:

> *'Then Hannah prayed and said: My heart rejoices in the Lord; in the Lord, my horn is lifted high. My mouth boasts over my enemies, for I delight in your deliverance. There is no one holy like the Lord. There is no one besides you. There is no Rock like our God."*

The Bible says, "Hannah prayed and said ..." You would have expected that if it were a prayer, she would have "asked" but instead we find that she praised; she said, "my heart rejoices in the Lord, in the Lord my horn is lifted high, my mouth boasts over my enemies."

This is an example of appreciation in praying through praise. Don't forget that after Hannah prayed and Eli gave her a reassurance of an answered prayer, the Bible records that her countenance changed immediately even without seeing the physical manifestation of that prayer. She had believed that her prayers had been answered and this chronicles her testimony. It shows her trust in God and her appreciation and gratitude of what God had done for her.

We must learn not to act as if we contributed to our lives or that we are assistants to God. People tend to see themselves as helping God, thinking they contributed at least 50% to the process of their breakthrough, their healing or their blessings. We can read the story of Uzzah and the Ark of the Covenant found in 2 Samuel 6:1-7 and 1 Chronicles 13:9-12. It was a time when the total glory and gratitude should have been directed to God; but as the ark was being transported, the oxen pulling the cart stumbled, and Uzzah (a Levite) took hold of the ark. God's anger burned against Uzzah, and He struck him down, and he died. Uzzah thought it was his responsibility to save the integrity of God, (to do the 50% deal) but God needs no help and deserves our full glory. We must move away from such thoughts of helping or giving God half praise because the more we praise, bless and glorify God, the more we are blessed. We must learn to bless those around us, our family, church members, pastors, and general overseers.

We must learn to dance and clap for what God had done and for that which He is doing of which we are even unaware. We must donate our lives to God, learn to lift others up.

Talking about the prophet that died in 2 Kings 4:1-7, appreciation may have been lacking in his life. For him to have been in a situation of lack; it may have been the lack of testifying to God's goodness. Maybe or may not.

As children of God, we need to be watchful that we are not going to get to a point of ingratitude but to a point of thankfulness.

Chapter 8: How to Make and Sustain Wealth by Appreciation

See Psalm 106:13-14,

> "Then they believed His words; they sang His praise. They quickly forgot His works; they did not wait for His counsel, but craved intensely in the wilderness, and tempted God in the desert."

This verse depicts what happened in Exodus 15, the children of Israel (led by Moses with a "Miriam and Moses song," got to the point of gratitude and expressed that gratitude through praise. However in that same chapter by the time they got to verse 24, they expressed the reversal of "gratitude" a 'grumble' act. So the people grumbled against Moses, saying, "What are we to drink?"

Even though God overlooked this occurrence (Exodus 15:26-27), He said,

> "If you listen carefully to the Lord your God and do what is right in his eyes, if you pay attention to his commands and keep all his decrees, I will not bring on you any of the diseases I brought on the Egyptians, for I am the Lord, who heals you." 27 Then they came to Elim, where there were twelve springs and seventy palm trees, and they camped there near the water."

The children of Israel still continued in failing to grasp the essence of thanks, and as a result, they experienced the results of ingratitude Numbers 14:20-23.

> "All the Israelites grumbled against Moses and Aaron, and the whole assembly said to them, "If only we had died in Egypt or in this wilderness!"

This act of being ungrateful was a costly one to them, even though God forgave them. The Lord replied,

> "I have forgiven them, as you asked. 21 Nevertheless, as surely as I live and as surely as the glory of the Lord fills the whole earth, 22 not one of those who saw my glory and the signs I performed in Egypt and in the wilderness but who disobeyed me and tested me ten times – 23 not one of them will ever see the land I promised on oath to their ancestors. No one who has treated me with contempt will ever see it."

If we truly seek for a triumph in the area of wealth, we must move far away from grumbling, taking on a more in-depth place in the act and art of showing gratitude.

We can see many more examples of how gratitude and appreciation to God brought about greater blessings - Luke 1:46, Mary said my soul magnifies God. You can appreciate God through your soul and spirit just like Mary and Hannah.

Wherever Abraham, Isaac, and Jacob went, they would build altars in appreciation to God. In Genesis 20:7, God appeared to Abraham and made him a covenant; Abraham built an altar to appreciate God. Hebrews 12:22 says, when you come to God you have come into an innumerable company of angels. Anytime we come to God; He will see it as appreciating Him.

Chapter 8: How to Make and Sustain Wealth by Appreciation

Abraham, Isaac, Meshach, Shadrach, Abednego, Joseph and Jacob did it. All my days I will appreciate you, I will worship you, I cannot miss the company of many angels.

When you appreciate God, it is very easy to appreciate your customers.

Let us consider the story of Noah as a showcase of appreciation:

See Gen 8:20-25.

> *"Then Noah built an altar to the Lord, and took of every clean animal and of every clean bird, and offered burnt offerings on the altar. 20 And the Lord smelled a soothing aroma. Then the Lord said in His heart, "I will never again curse the ground for man's sake, although the imagination of man's heart is evil from his youth; nor will I again destroy every living thing as I have done." 22 "While the earth remains, Seedtime and harvest, Cold and heat, winter and summer, and day and night shall not cease."*

Just by the act of appreciation, God changed His mind. We as individuals can bring God to change His mind. You can alter the course of your life at the altar of appreciation.

When we appreciate and acknowledge God in our wealth making process, God gives us new ideas and more opportunities to make more wealth.

We go back to one of my favourite verses Deuteronomy 8:18, the message version, says

> "If you start thinking to yourselves, "I did all this. And all by myself. I'm rich. It's all mine!" – well, think again. Remember that God, your God, gave you the strength to produce all this wealth so as to confirm the covenant that He promised to your ancestors – as it is today."

New King James Version states:

> "And you shall remember the Lord your God, for it is He who gives you power to get wealth that He may establish His covenant which He swore to your fathers, as it is this day."

HOW CAN APPRECIATION BE SHOWN?

1. BY SHARING YOUR TESTIMONY

There are three things about sharing testimonies.

- Are you sharing with humility?
- Always remember you were once in the wilderness.
- And it is God that brought you out.

If God wants to open a door to you, you will, in all probabilities, go through a test. When you pass the test, God gives a testimony (See the story of Joseph). That is why Joseph said to his brothers, if it were left to you, I would have been dead (Genesis 50:20). God sees your heart and knows if you obey Him. The act of sharing your testimony is an act of appreciation, and in doing this God, God gives you more wealth. When Mary was visited by

Chapter 8: How to Make and Sustain Wealth by Appreciation

the angel and given her word, she went to visit Elizabeth, who in turn, encouraged Mary by her prophecy.

See Luke 1:39-56;

When you share your testimonies with one another, not only are you giving thanks, you are also building the faith of one another.

However, we must ensure that we do not share a premature testimony. We must also make sure that we keep a check on our tongue from being reckless with our testimonies. Your testimony must be properly baked before being shared. You must ensure you are not eating too soon before your cake is baked. Luke 2:19 tells us that Mary kept it in her heart and thought about them often (See Daniel 7:28). Daniel showed maturity. He kept the matter to himself.

> *"This is the end of the matter. I, Daniel, was deeply troubled by my thoughts, and my face turned pale, but I kept the matter to myself."*

You may ask the question 'how exactly would I know it is the right time to share my testimony?'

There are two ways of knowing a mature testimony:

- The boldness and the confidence in sharing.
- Having an assurance that your testimony will convict and minister to someone.

Testimony is not about telling a story. It is about acknowledging what God did to turn a situation around and explaining to people that just as God did it for me, He will do it for you. See the woman of Samaria in John 4: 28-30,

> *"Then, leaving her water jar, the woman went back to the town and said to the people, 29 "Come, see a man who told me everything I ever did. Could this be the Messiah?" 30 They came out of the town and made their way toward him."*

See verse 39 and 42,

> *"Many of the Samaritans from that town believed in him because of the woman's testimony, "He told me everything I ever did. So when the Samaritans came to him, they urged him to stay with them, and he stayed two days. And because of his words, many more became believers. They said to the woman, 'We no longer believe just because of what you said; now we have heard for ourselves, and we know that this man really is the Saviour of the world."*

These must be the essence of your testimony. Reckless mouth and too much unguarded words are wrong. Don't share a testimony and boast of what you have done wrong to get a conceived profit.

Watch your mouth and be careful with whom you discuss your marriage, business and future.

Chapter 8: How to Make and Sustain Wealth by Appreciation

In Galatians 1:15-17, Apostle Paul refused to discuss his destiny with anyone.

> *"But when it pleased God, who separated me from my mother's womb and called me through His grace, to reveal His Son in me, that I might preach Him among the Gentiles, I did not immediately confer with flesh and blood, nor did I go up to Jerusalem to those who were apostles before me; but I went to Arabia, and returned again to Damascus."*

There are things the devil does not know, that God told you. If you spread them, the devil can use them against you.

See also 2 Kings 20:12-19. This is where Hezekiah opened up his house and other properties to the envoys from Babylon. He suffered for it.

> *"At that time Berodach-Baladan a son of Baladan, king of Babylon, sent letters and a gift to Hezekiah, for he had heard that Hezekiah had been sick. Hezekiah listened to and welcomed them and foolishly showed them all his treasure house - the silver and gold and spices and precious oil and his armoury and everything that was found in his treasuries. There was nothing in his house (palace) nor in all his realm that Hezekiah did not show them. Then Isaiah the prophet came to King Hezekiah and said to him, "What did these men say [that would cause you to do this for them]? From where have they come to you?" Hezekiah said, "They have come from a far country, from Babylon." Isaiah said, "What have they seen in your house?" Hezekiah answered, "They have seen*

everything that is in my house (palace). There is nothing in my treasuries that I have not shown them." Then Isaiah said to Hezekiah, *"Hear the word of the Lord. 17 Behold, the time is coming when everything that is in your house, and that your fathers have stored up until this day, will be carried to Babylon; nothing will be left,' says the Lord. 18 And some of your sons (descendants) who will be born to you will be taken away [as captives]; and they will become eunuchs in the palace of the king of Babylon.'"* Then Hezekiah said to Isaiah, *"The word of the Lord which you have spoken is good."* For he thought, *"Is it not good, if [at least] there will be peace and security in my lifetime?"*

The Bible also tells us that,

> *"Whoever guards his mouth and tongue keeps his soul from troubles"* (Proverbs 21:23 NKJV).

> *"Do not trust in a friend; Do not put your confidence in a companion; Guard the doors of your mouth from her who lies in your bosom"* (Micah 7:5 NKJV).

2. THROUGH A TESTIMONIAL

See Roman 16 1-2,

> *"I commend to you Phoebe our sister, who is a servant of the church in Cenchrea, 2 that you may receive her in the Lord in a manner worthy of the saints, and assist her in whatever business she has need of you; for indeed she has been a helper of many and of myself also."*

Chapter 8: How to Make and Sustain Wealth by Appreciation

Also see 1Corinthians 16:17- 18,

> "I rejoice over the coming of Stephanas and Fortunatus and Achaicus, because they have supplied what was lacking on your part. For they have refreshed my spirit and yours. Therefore acknowledge such men."

Here Paul appreciated individuals for what they have done. He did not take the view that they could read his mind or God will reward them. He publically acknowledged them and appreciated them.

And in 2 Timothy 1:15-17 Paul asked for mercy for the household of Onesiphorus. He appreciated Onesiphorus for his support and of the brethren in Asia, he was direct in telling of their shortfall.

> "This you know, that all those in Asia have turned away from me, among whom are Phygellus and Hermogenes. The Lord grant mercy to the household of Onesiphorus, for he often refreshed me, and was not ashamed of my chain; but when he arrived in Rome, he sought me out very zealously and found me."

3. EXPRESS APPRECIATION DIRECTLY TO THE INDIVIDUAL

We read of how Ruth expressed and showed appreciation in Ruth 2:10, and in her showing such appreciation, she gained more see verse 12

> "Then she fell on her face, bowing to the ground, and said to him, "Why have I found favour in your eyes,

that you should take notice of me, since I am a foreigner?" 11 But Boaz answered her, "All that you have done for your mother-in-law since the death of your husband has been fully told to me, and how you left your father and mother and your native land and came to a people that you did not know before. 12 The Lord repay you for what you have done, and a full reward be given you by the Lord, the God of Israel, under whose wings you have come to take refuge!"

4. YOU CAN GIVE A PUBLIC APPRECIATION

In 2 Thessalonians 1, Paul gave a public appreciation of the church of Thessalonians. He acknowledged their growing faith and the faith that he took pleasure in; boasting about their faith.

Paul was also a great appreciator of God. In 1 Timothy 1:12-17, we see Paul appreciating Christ for calling him into ministry:

"And I thank Christ Jesus our Lord who has enabled me, because He counted me faithful, putting me into the ministry, 13 although I was formerly a blasphemer, a persecutor, and an insolent man; but I obtained mercy because I did it ignorantly in unbelief. 14 And the grace of our Lord was exceedingly abundant, with faith and love which are in Christ Jesus. 15 This is a faithful saying and worthy of all acceptance, that Christ Jesus came into the world to save sinners, of whom I am chief"

And in Mark 9:7 God appreciated and acknowledged Jesus

> *"And a cloud overshadowed them, and a voice came out of the cloud, "This is my beloved Son; listen to him."*

Once you master how to appreciate God; it is not difficult to master how to appreciate man's good deeds in your business, place of work, ministry and in all endeavours of life.

WHEN AND HOW DO YOU APPRECIATE?

- We must appreciate people at every opportunity we have (1 Thessalonians 5:18; John 13: 34-35).

- When you wake up, and you feel yourself, appreciate God (2 Timothy 4:14-15; 1 Chronicles 16:34).

- When you want to pray for someone, you can appreciate them (1 Corinth 1:4-5).

- When you want to start your business, the best strategy is first to appreciate God (Psalm 100:4).

- Even in your office appreciate God under your breath (Psalm 150:6).

- You appreciate people to encourage them (2 Timothy 4:20-24).

- You can do it by teaching others to do the same or by showing your gratitude.

CONCLUSION

Gratitude is the measure of altitude. The opposite of appreciation is condemnation. Appreciate your clients and customers. Let them know you honour and love their custom. Let them feel welcome at all times. Ensure that your customer service ranks as the best in town. Thank them when they pay your fees. Do not take it for granted. You cannot litter negativity everywhere and wonder why you have got a trash of a life. Don't despise the days of humble beginning. Anyone that asks what this is will remain as it is. The children of Israel said "what is this?" at the manna God gave them and for that, it took them 40 years of hardship. That will not be your portion in Jesus name. Many people who murmur and grumble are always sad and mean because they do not know how to appreciate. However, God calls us to give thanks in everything at all times.

Chapter 9

Life Learning Building Block - The Practical Art of Making and Keeping Money

THE TIDBITS

It is essential in life to learn about money. God wants us to know about the principles, and be custodians of godly wealth. This chapter outlines how to engage in the practical art of making and keeping money.

Before going into the practicalities of making money, four fundamental principles must be learned and mastered. An individual seeking for godly wealth must begin by knowing and abiding by them. These are:

1. UNLOVE ANY LOVE YOU HAVE FOR MONEY

The Bible tells us that the love of money is the root of all kinds of evil (see 1 Timothy 6:10). Note that it is the love of money, not money in itself. By implication, this means that money is relevant, important and needs to be considered very seriously. However, it is choosing to love it that is bad.

By not loving money but considering and using money wisely, you can make money your servant. For a wise man, money should indeed be a great servant that can be sent forth to bring about our prosperity and to bring about the building of God's kingdom. By the same token, if money is loved it becomes a harsh master.

2. KNOW THAT YOU ARE THE CUSTODIAN OF MONEY; NOT MONEY BEING YOUR CUSTODIAN

The reason for God blessing us with wealth is made clear in Deuteronomy 8:18,

> *"And you shall remember the Lord your God, for it is He who gives you power to get wealth that He may establish His covenant which He swore to your fathers, as it is this day."*

In the financial sector, a custodian is described as 'a financial institution that holds customers' securities for safekeeping so as to minimise the risk of theft or loss.' A custodian holds securities and other assets in electronic or physical form. We can safely conclude that, firstly, it is God who gives the power to make wealth and, secondly, the power to make wealth is given for the purpose of fulfilling and establishing a covenant.

The essence of God giving the power and establishing His covenant denotes a process of God passing onto an individual a gift or ability. As such, that individual does not own that power; God gives it to them for a purpose.

Moreover, in effect, that individual has become a custodian - they hold a "trusted role." God therefore, will seek and watch to see how much the individual can be trusted with and how the individual will put his gift to use.

The more God trusts you, the more He commits His wealth and power into your custody because he has seen that you will not misuse it.

3. UNDERSTANDING THE NEED TO BE CONSIDERED AT ALL TIMES

Proverbs 15:14 says,

> *"The heart of him who has understanding seeks knowledge, but the mouth of fools feed on foolishness."*

As an individual seeking for financial triumph, you must look well at all issues before making a decision about any money venture or in fact any venture at all.

Wealthy people are studious and conscious of where to invest and how they use their money. God does not commit money into the hands of lazy or carefree people. We can see this in the parable of the talents.

> *14-18 "It's also like a man going off on an extended trip. He called his servants together and delegated responsibilities. To one he gave five thousand dollars, to another two thousand, to a third one thousand, depending on their abilities. Then he left. Right off,*

the first servant went to work and doubled his master's investment. The second did the same. But the man with the single thousand dug a hole and carefully buried his master's money.

19-21 "After a long absence, the master of those three servants came back and settled up with them. The one given five thousand dollars showed him how he had doubled his investment. His master commended him: 'Good work! You did your job well. From now on be my partner.'

22-23 "The servant with the two thousand showed how he also had doubled his master's investment. His master commended him: 'Good work! You did your job well. From now on be my partner.'

24-25 "The servant given one thousand said, 'Master, I know you have high standards and hate careless ways that you demand the best and make no allowances for error. I was afraid I might disappoint you, so I found a good hiding place and secured your money. Here it is, safe and sound down to the last cent.'

26-27 "The master was furious. 'That's a terrible way to live! It's criminal to live cautiously like that! If you knew I was after the best, why did you do less than the least? The least you could have done would have been to invest the sum with the bankers, where at least I would have gotten a little interest.

28-30 "'Take the thousand and give it to the one who risked the most. And get rid of this "play-it-safe" who won't go out on a limb. Throw him out into utter darkness." (Matthew 25:14-30 (MSG))

4. YOU MUST NOT BURY YOUR TALENTS

At all times, you must seek to, build and empower your legacy. Ecclesiastes 9:10 says

> *"Whatever your hand finds to do, do it with your might; for there is no work or device or knowledge or wisdom in the grave where you are going."*

Take a look at those who make money and keep it; they are people who maximise their potentials, gifts, and abilities. Once these foundational principles are set and embedded in you, you can then begin planning how you wish to approach this. You will always have a starting point in the process of wealth making; it is the point of "where am I right now?"

It could be that you are in a position of lack or a position of just wanting an increase, the same practical principles will apply. No one is too young or too old in seeking for financial breakthrough. Your starting point must generate a degree of self-reflection. Some of the questions you ask yourself may include:

1. How do I start to make money?
2. How do I multiply the money I have?
3. How do I control my expenditures?
4. How do I guard the money saved from loss?

5. How do I own my property and keep making money from it?

6. How do I ensure a future income for future generations?

7. How do I increase my ability to earn more? And,

8. Where is God in all of this?

Let's go back to our core text in 2 Kings 4, focusing now on verses 2-7,

> *Elisha said, "I wonder how I can be of help. Tell me, what do you have in your house?"*
>
> *"Nothing," she said. "Well, I do have a little oil."*
>
> *"Here's what you do," said Elisha. "Go up and down the street and borrow jugs and bowls from all your neighbours. And not just a few – all you can get. Then come home and lock the door behind you, you and your sons. Pour oil into each container; when each is full, set it aside."*
>
> *She did what he said. She locked the door behind her and her sons; and as they brought the containers to her, she filled them. When all the jugs and bowls were full, she said to one of her sons, "Another jug, please."*
>
> *He said, "That's it. There are no more jugs."*

We see from this passage, so many helpful pointers including the freedom to choose and explore from within oneself.

Chapter 9: Life Learning Building Block - The Practical Art of Making and Keeping Money

Elisha said, "I wonder how I can help, tell me what you have." The widow could have stopped at the first word in her response, that is, "nothing" but then she remembered the oil. Again, in verses 5-6 she could have stopped at "two jugs," but she kept bringing out more jugs.

This tells us that there are choices we make in life. Anyone who wants to make money and have a peaceful future should be a self-questioning individual. Keep asking yourself:

- What have I been created for (see Jeremiah 1:1-5)?

- What are the things I have now? What kind of life do I want to live? The kind of life you want to live will determine how much work you put into life. The more you put in, the more you benefit from it.

- Where do I want to live? Do you plan to live in a big, nice house? Then you need to work hard and smart.

- What sort of schools do I want my children to attend? Do I want my children to attend the best schools, private and independent? Then, it is not for the faint-hearted. Think and plan now.

- What kind of holidays do I want to have? If you love exotic white beaches, yacht, and other nice stuff on vacation – you have to work towards it being able to afford it without going into debt.

- What sort of philanthropy will I support? Alternatively, is it that you would love to give generously to the work of God and other charitable works? Whatever you prefer, you will need more than prayer, and you also need to avoid careless playing or spending.

- How do you want your time managed? Do you want to keep clocking in or do you want to have absolute control of your own time?

- What kind of retirement do you want to have and at what age? If you do not want to work from the cradle to the grave; then be alive to what you need to do now.

- How much do you want to live on in retirement? If you do not want to rely on the State, and queue at the dole shop, snap out of bed now and put your strength to making money now.

None of the above questions is unscriptural, and anyone on a trip to financial triumph will do well to reflect on them. As this chapter deals with practical tips, let us now focus on practical and everyday living tips to work with.

Chapter 9: Life Learning Building Block - The Practical Art of Making and Keeping Money

HOW DO YOU START WITH YOUR FINANCES?

This is your best question and a start to your financial discipline. Start out by strictly allocating what comes in; do not compromise on this regardless of the amount.

1. 10% OF YOUR INCOME IS FOR GOD - TITHES

This is essential. I consider this a loving commandment: You shall truly tithe all the increase of your grain that the field produces year by year. It shall be done without a grudge and in love towards the Lord. (Deuteronomy 14:22)

2. A THIRD FOR SAVINGS (30%) - YOUR SEED

Never spend all and never eat your seed. It is best practice to save 30% of your income. See the story of Joseph.

And in the seven plenteous years, the earth brought forth by handfuls. Moreover, he gathered up all the food of the seven years, which were in the land of Egypt, and laid up the food in the cities: the food of the field, which was round about every city, laid him up in the same. And Joseph gathered corn as the sand of the sea, very much, until he left numbering; for it was without number.

3. THE REST TO SPEND (60%)

You are free to spend the rest on a need basis rather than a want basis. The idea is to have more savings in your portfolio rather than spending more that you earn but God still expects you to enjoy life, and to enjoy the things he has blessed you with. See 1 Timothy 6:17:

> *"Charge them that are rich in this world, that they be not high-minded, nor trust in uncertain riches, but in the living God, who gives us richly all things to enjoy."*

It is also a good habit to record what you spend on and how much you spend. Robert Frost said, "nobody was ever meant to remember or invent what he has ever spent." So it is best to write down your spending. Master where you are spending it. His formula can be adapted as you master the art of spending and saving.

THREE FUNDAMENTAL KINDS OF SAVINGS

1. SAVINGS TO SPEND

This is an 'emergency fund.' This is a build-up of money you set aside or reserve only for emergency, say between £1000 and £20,000 depending on your earning power.

Chapter 9: Life Learning Building Block - The Practical Art of Making and Keeping Money

2. NORMAL SAVINGS

This can be an endowment, cash ISA, fixed deposit et cetera. These are monies that, no matter the emergency, you do not spend. The idea is to see these savings grow. It is your feel good factor.

3. INVESTMENTS AND BUSINESS

These are of longer term savings and include investments such as stocks, stocks ISAs, property, bonds et cetera. These have some element of risk and will depend on the level of risk you are willing to take. This group can bring you real financial breakthrough, if you are smart, but can also break you, so be careful and get independent financial advice before investing in any financial product.

COMMON ENEMIES TO SAVINGS

These are some very fundamental common enemies to savings, and you will be amazed at how these things serve as hindrances to you building up a pot of gold.

- Clothes - not that you should be naked, but have a reasonable limit and do not waste money.
- Food and drink – again, not that you should be hungry and thirsty, spend wisely. Instead of always buying lunch at work, take food from home. I know of

a woman who often packs rice and stew (or whatever food at home) for her lunch at work to save money. Despite her colleagues being able to afford eating out every day, they often wish they had her lunches instead. Similarly, at home, avoid having takeaways too often. Cook your meals in bulk and portion them into the freezer for daily use. Likewise, avoid using the local convenience store for your food shopping, use the supermarkets for your bulk shopping and your local store for emergency top ups such as milk or bread.

- Entertainment - Be careful of spending too much money on entertainment. There are many free or inexpensive family fun day outs in each borough. Also, take advantage of discounted leisure activities and off peak holidays.

- Toys for children and the 'boys' smart sports car, gadgets, wristwatches etc. - These can lead to financial ruin

- Bad habits – such as smoking, gambling, and excessive drinking. They are detrimental to your wellbeing and expensive! Put the money for such habits into a tin for one month and see just how much you have accumulated in that time.

- Re-mortgaging for the sake of unplanned spending

Chapter 9: Life Learning Building Block - The Practical Art of Making and Keeping Money

- Credit Cards and Store Cards – whenever and wherever you see the word 'credit,' replace it with 'debt.' So, it is a 'debt card,' not a credit card.
- Hire Purchase
- Overspending during festive periods
- Borrowing for non-investment or non-business purposes – why do it? Live within your means and not to impress others. Remember Proverbs 22:7; a borrower is a servant to the lender.

CONTROLLING EXPENDITURE

Once you have eliminated the enemies of savings listed above, you then need to ask yourself "How do I multiply my earnings?"

1. The first thing you need to do is to stop borrowing either from the bank or people. Just stop borrowing. Live within your means.
2. Keep short term liabilities
3. Develop a habit of regular savings. For example, as soon as you can, you should invest in an ISA, you are never too young to do so.
4. Have some investment that gradually increases in value - create a pot of gold for important events
5. Know how to master your necessities and desires

6. Turn habits into money - are you good in some habits, walking a dog or plaiting hair for friends, stop doing it all for free.

Invest in stocks. It is said that Warren Buffett's financial strategy was to be fearful when others are greedy but greedy when others are fearful. That is to buy at the time of maximum pessimism and sell at the time of minimum optimism.

Also, we need to move from earner to saver to an investor to a philanthropist. It is said that Warren Buffet gave away billions of dollars to charities run by Bill Gates.

MY PERSONAL FORMULA - ESSI (EARN SPEND SAVE INVEST)

I have a formula that guides me: It is called ESSI - Earn, Spend, Save, and Invest. You cannot run away from earning as sure as you cannot run away from spending. The possibility of spending more, the more you earn is real! So you need to fashion your adaptable strategy of how to save and invest what you have earned before you finish spending it all.

There is always a reward for saving. A simple saving plan I read somewhere states that if you keep £300 every month in a savings account with compound interest for 30 years, you should have approximately £300,000. These principles will help you control your spending habits:

Chapter 9: Life Learning Building Block - The Practical Art of Making and Keeping Money

- Don't go on a spending spree
- Have regular savings
- Have a property by age 28, anywhere in the world
- Have shares that gradually grow
- Have a pot of gold for your children's wedding. By the time they are getting married, they will not struggle
- Know how to master your necessities
- Don't worry what you suffer now; you will enjoy later. There is a time of saving and also a time of harvest.

WEALTHY WAYS

Chapter 10

Prayers

I do not know what your age is, and as you may be aware, age does not create a limit to God. Abraham was 75 years old when God entered into his life (Genesis 12:4). Moses was 80 years old when he began his journey to deliver the children of Israel (Exodus 7:7). On the other hand, according to the Bible, Methuselah (Genesis 5:27), the longest/oldest living human according to the Bible, did not achieve anything tangible. In contrast to him, Enoch, his father, who lived only a third of his son's life (Genesis 5:23-24), achieved a significant legacy.

Anyone that has experienced delayed success in any matter because of their age can experience supernatural speed by the power that is in the name of Jesus. Pray for supernatural speed, accomplishment, and prosperity. Pray that God delivers you from enemies disguised as friends. Keep on praying for yourself, and you are invited to use the list below to help you raise specific issues to God.

- Even if you have just £1, speak prophetically to that money today, just like the widow of Zarephath, say of that money, 'your container of flour will not be empty, its oil will not be dry.'
- Just like the boy that gave five loaves of bread and two fish and still had plenty baskets remaining, speak to the money that you have and declare that the money will not run dry in the mighty name of Jesus. Declare that there is provision for you to take care of your marriage, children and family.
- Declare that you will not lack in the mighty name of Jesus.
- Let every woman declare that she will not lack in the mighty name of Jesus.
- From today, every dryness that has crept into my life, I command it to receive water today, let the rain of blessings fall, and let the showers of blessings fall in the mighty name of Jesus.
- The Bible tells me that the tongue of the righteous is like a choice silver, as a business person, as I speak customers will be favouring me.
- The Bible tells me that the path of the righteous shines brighter and brighter every day. I say from this moment everyone in the corridors of power that should bless me, every gatekeeper, every gate opener, and every door opener that sets their eyes, or their

thoughts upon me, will hurry to bless me in the mighty name of Jesus.

- If I am unemployed, I say that I am headhunted for great roles and positions. Employers will be chasing me for good reasons.
- All my wasted effort has become gainful effort.
- I banish every agony of sin, every spirit of iniquity, every greed and every pride that has buffeted me for so long and has made me stay at the base of the mountain for so long;
- For husbands and wives: Pray that money will not be an issue for us again in the mighty name of Jesus.
- For those who pay school fees: As I am paying for this term, the one for the next is already in my pocket.
- For employees: As I earn my salary, I cut off every devourer that will want to take that money in the mighty name of Jesus.
- As I purpose in my heart to give money for offerings and tithes, God will open doors that cannot be closed.
- I have hearing ears to understand when He speaks to me. He gives me great ideas that move me away from the ordinary to the supernatural.
- The end has come for lack in my life, the siege is over, and I am walking into my glorious abundance in the

mighty name of Jesus. Every curse is lifted by God for my sake in Jesus' name.

- Every redemption that is not yet complete in my life shall be speedily complete today in the mighty name of Jesus.
- Every spirit of the prowler, every spirit of the armed man that is preventing me from reaching my God-given destiny; turn back right now in the mighty name of Jesus.
- The hand of the ungodly and the hand of bad news, which is seeking to come upon me like a prowler is withered in the mighty name of Jesus.
- From today the mystery of God's divine blessing will be made clear to me in the mighty name of Jesus.
- From today, as I continually say it, I will continually see it, as I continually observe to do, God will continually embarrass me with blessings.
- Every one of my gifts or calling that is associated with prosperity that has not been seen by me or that has not materialised in my life or that the enemy has killed, in the mighty name of Jesus, receives repentance today.
- From today I will be poor no more.
- The joy of His kingdom wealth comes upon my head, Amen.

Chapter 10: Prayers

- As the anointing of the Holy Spirit brings me into the powerful blessedness of God's kingdom wealth, every time-waster, devourer, every power that sees negativity today will turn back and run away from me.

- From today, instead of curses, I shall be blessed, I will be delighted in the Lord in the mighty name of Jesus.

- I speak to my finances from today, wherever they are saying there is bankruptcy or there is falling down, wherever they are pulling me down, and it is not enough, I say I will not be found there in the mighty name of Jesus.

- I will have great ideas in the mighty name of Jesus.

- If like Isaac in Genesis 26:12, I am a migrant in the country I currently live in, I receive favour and blessings. Just like the Philistines envied Isaac but could not hinder his blessings, I too, am envied because of God's blessings upon me and no one will be able to hinder my blessings in Jesus' name, Amen.

- I am beginning to prosper; I will continue to prosper, and I will be very prosperous.

- As I continue in this new season of financial triumph, I receive my breakthrough. Some have received theirs, and mine has started.

- Whatever the Lord needs to do to bring me into my financial destiny, into my financial accomplishment, He will do now in the mighty name of Jesus.

66 SCRIPTURAL NUGGETS TO FINANCIAL BREAKTHROUGH

The previous chapters dealt with core traits on which to lay the foundation of financial breakthrough; helping to confirm that triumphing in finances takes a lot of discipline and virtues.

This chapter will look at scriptures in the bible that you can stand on to break the barrier of financial bondage. These scriptures will open your mind to the reality that God is interested in your prosperity.

God's Word is the manual to financial success you can count on, and stand on every word.

Nugget 1

Understand the Purpose of Wealth

Consider Deuteronomy 8:6-18, and in particular, see verse 18 which says *'and you shall remember the Lord your God, for it is he who gives you power to get wealth that he may establish his covenant which he swore to your fathers, as it is this day.'*

So the purpose of wealth is first to provide for your family and then to use it to support God's work (for example, through church planting, charities, etc.).

Nugget 2

Understand God's position in relation to wealth

According to Deuteronomy 28:2-14, God's allocation for us is that of blessings. Furthermore, with reference to Deuteronomy 28:15; Proverbs 10:15; 6:9, poverty only emerges as a curse. However, God has already provided a solution to this, and other curses. Have a look at Galatians 3:13-14 and 16-19:

> *"Christ has redeemed us from the curse of the law having become a curse for us that the blessing of Abraham might come upon the Gentiles in Christ Jesus."*

God's plan for us is not just to have wealth and success but to have good success as seen in Joshua 1:7-8,

> *'Thou shall have good success'. Prosperity is not just money; it's about not failing. It is a real promise linked to the essence of experiencing all round peace. God's plan for is to have all round prosperity (3 John 1:2).*

Nugget 3

Understand the art and of act seeding

The parable of The Sower in Luke 8:4-8 helps us understand the biblical act of seeding. It is paramount that you be a 'sower.' Characteristics of being a sower are:

- A sower is always a reaper; but a reaper may not necessarily be a sower, because you may be a hired reaper.

- A sower is always better than a reaper (better to give than to receive)

- The harvest is usually proportionate to the seed that is sown.

- A sower determines where he sows; he may not be able to determine what comes out of the seed. What comes out of the ground is dependent on many things; conditions of ground, bypass, thorns, rock, good ground, and inevitably God (see Luke 16 concerning the unjust steward and also Luke 15 concerning the parables of 'The lost sheep', 'The Lost Coin' and 'The Lost Son').

Nugget 4

Understand how to sow your seed and the fact that your seed is for prospering

The commitment you put into seeking the seed and guiding it, is proportionate to the value you attach to the seed. In Zechariah 8:12 we see that,

> *"The seed shall be prosperous. The vine shall give his fruit."*

There are four main ways in which your seed, which is often your income, may be given (seeded/planted):

- Tithing. Please note that this is compulsory for every Christian (see Genesis 14:19, Proverbs 3:9-10 Malachi 3:7-12).

- As an offering - Although offerings are voluntary, I highly recommended Christians to give these. The amount you give is up to you (see 2 Corinthians 9:10-12).

- Alms which are also voluntary but recommended (see Acts 10:1-2).

- A vow or sacrificial giving which God always responds to (see 1 Kings 17:8-16).

Other types of giving include:

  - Giving to the poor (Proverbs 19:17);

- Giving to a friend, or give on behalf of a friend (1 John 3:16, 1 John 3:17).

- Giving according to the principle of Hebrews 7:7; *'without doubt, the lesser is blessed by the greater';*

- Giving to your spouse and children or giving an offering to God on their behalf (Ephesians 5:25);

- Giving to parents or giving to God on their behalf (1 Timothy 5:8);

- You can give to a prophet (Matt 10:41-42);

- Give to a building fund (Psalm 102:13-14 and 1 Chronicles 29:7-9);

- Giving an offering to a church (Luke 6:38);

- Give a pledge or a vow (Psalm 66:13).

Nugget 5

Understand the principles of activating wealth

Psalm 112:1, 3

> *"Praise ye the Lord, Blessed is the man that feareth the Lord; that delighted greatly in his commandments. Wealth and riches shall be in his house, and his righteousness endureth forever."*

How you are spiritually, affect how you are financially (3 John 1:2). The principles of wealth activation are discussed in the earlier chapters of this book.

Nugget 6

Understand that God takes pleasure in your prosperity

"God has pleasure in the prosperity of his servants" (Psalm 35:27).

He loves it when you proper.

Nugget 7

Understand the "Know-how of continuous prosperity."

Genesis 26:12

"Then Isaac sowed in that Land, and reaped in the same year a hundredfold, and the Lord blessed him. The man began to prosper, and continued prospering until he became prosperous."

The more difficult your circumstance is, the more opportunity you have to prosper. For example, the widow of Zarephath (1Kings 17:8-16). It was a difficult time for her, but she took a step of faith and prospered all around.

God's covenant of blessing and prosperity is not dependent on your situation or the environment. God can open any closed door in your life (Proverbs 16:7).

Your enemies shall be your friends when God's blessings begin to chase and overtake you. For example, when I began as a Pastor, some of my friends did not understand how I could take such a step and they thought that I would not be successful and that it would be a temporary phase. However, the further I became entrenched in the ministry, the more God has blessed me.

Nugget 8

Understand the fact that your tongue can bring you into wealth

"The tongue of the righteous is choice silver; the heart of the wicked is worth little" (Proverbs 10:20).

What you declare is what you receive. Whatever you call yourself is what you shall become. If you say you are poor, yes you are, but if you say you can never be poor, you shall not be poor.

Nugget 9

Understand that the blessings of God make rich and, it adds no sorrow

"The blessing of the Lord makes one rich, and he adds no sorrow with it" (Proverbs 10:20-22).

When God is the one blessing you, you can go to bed. It is certain that such blessings cannot bring ill-health or sadness. Such blessings cannot cause you sleeplessness.

Nugget 10

God blessings are overflowing; He supplies every need

"He is able to do exceedingly and abundantly more that we think or ask" (Ephesians 3:20).

"My God shall supply all my needs according to his riches in Glory in Christ Jesus" (Philippians 4:19).

Imagine the extent of your asking and the thoughts. With this scripture you can buy a private jet, whilst driving a Volkswagen! This scripture takes you away from where you are to where you should be.

Nugget 11

God's blessings and wealth are based on set principles

> "Give, and it shall be given to you, good measure, Pressed down, shaken together, running over, same measure you use, shall be measured back to you" (Luke 6:38).

I love this. It is a confident kind of prayer. It should push you to sow and to give. You cannot out-give God.

Nugget 12

Righteousness brings about prosperity

> "He shall be like a tree planted by the rivers of water that brings forth its fruit in its season whose leaf also shall not wither and whatever he does shall prosper" (Psalms 1:3).

- To be prosperous, you must be well rooted.
- To be prosperous, you must be watered and watered continuously (by river)
- Prosperity is wealth accessed when needed in its season.
- There is every produce for every period.

Nugget 13

The blessing of prosperity is fully rounded

The Book of Malachi describes the fully rounded seven blessings of tithing (Malachi 3:10-12):

- Revival
- Abundance
- The enemy vanquished
- Fruit protected
- A testimony of God's goodness
- Family protected
- Chosen for service

Nugget 14

The blessing of prosperity can be activated through FAVOUR

As we can see in Exodus 12:36, the Lord gave the Israelites favour with the Egyptians so that they granted them what they requested. In this way, the Israelites plundered the Egyptians before the left the Egypt.

Nugget 15

The blessing of prosperity can be activated through obedience and assurances

Leviticus 26:3-6

"If you walk in My statutes and keep My commandments, and perform them, then I will give you rain in its season, the land shall yield its produce, and the trees of the field shall yield their fruit. Your threshing shall last till the time of vintage, and the vintage shall last till the time of sowing; you shall eat your bread to the full, and dwell in your land safely. I will give peace in the land, and you shall lie down, and none will make you afraid; I will rid the land of evil beasts, and the sword will not go through your land."

Nugget 16

The blessing of prosperity is a sure one - an assurance blessing

Numbers 23: 19-20

"God is not a man, that He should lie, nor a son of man, that He should repent. Has He said, and will He not do? Or has He spoken, and will He not make it good? Behold, I have received a command to bless; He has blessed, and I cannot reverse it."

Nugget 17

You can set up a contract with God by making a VOW

Judges 11:30-34

> *"And Jephthah made a vow to the Lord, and said, "If You will indeed deliver the people of Ammon into my hands, then it will be that whatever comes out of the doors of my house to meet me, when I return in peace from the people of Ammon, shall surely be the Lord's, and I will offer it up as a burnt offering." So Jephthah advanced toward the people of Ammon to fight against them, and the Lord delivered them into his hands. And he defeated them from Aroer as far as Minnith – twenty cities – and to Abel Keramim, with a very great slaughter. Thus the people of Ammon were subdued before the children of Israel. When Jephthah came to his house at Mizpah, there was his daughter, coming out to meet him with timbrels and dancing; and she was his only child. Besides her, he had neither son nor daughter."*

Nugget 18

The pursuit of pleasantness can activate the blessings of prosperity

> *"Wherever you go, I will go and wherever you lodge I will lodge, your people shall be my people, your God my God" (Ruth 1:16).*

In this passage, Ruth is speaking to her mother in law, Naomi. 'Naomi' is the Hebrew word for 'pleasant.' Ruth had determined in her heart to follow Naomi (pleasantness) wherever she went. Although they were both initially in dire straits, their lives turned out to be very pleasant.

Nugget 19

Building Godly friendships can activate the blessings of prosperity

See 1 Samuel 16:7-13 and 2 Samuel 22:33 for the example of friendship between David and Jonathan.

Nugget 20

Giving to the building of God's temple can activate the blessings of prosperity

1 Chronicles 29:7-9

> "They gave for the work of the house of God five thousand talents and ten thousand darics of gold, ten thousand talents of silver, eighteen thousand talents of bronze, and one hundred thousand talents of iron. And whoever had precious stones gave them to the treasury of the house of the Lord, into the hand of Jehiel the Gershonite. Then the people rejoiced, for they had offered willingly, because with a loyal heart

they had offered willingly to the Lord; and King David also rejoiced greatly."

Also see Psalm 102:13-14.

A leader in Israel, whose servant was sick got healing from Jesus, because the leaders of the synagogue gave a testimonial on his behalf that he built for them a synagogue. Get into the habit of building churches for God. You cannot fail (Luke 7:1-10).

Nugget 21

Faith giving can activate the blessings of prosperity

1 Kings 17:10-16

So she said, "As the Lord your God lives, I do not have bread, only a handful of flour in a bin, and a little oil in a jar; and see, I am gathering a couple of sticks that I may go in and prepare it for myself and my son, that we may eat it, and die. And Elijah said to her, "Do not fear; go and do as you have said, but make me a small cake from it first, and bring it to me; and afterward make some for yourself and your son. For thus says the Lord God of Israel: 'The bin of flour shall not be used up, nor shall the jar of oil run dry, until the day the Lord sends rain on the earth.' So she went away and did according to the word of Elijah; and she and he and her household ate for many days. The bin of flour was not used up, nor did the jar of oil run dry, according to the word of the Lord which He spoke by Elijah.

Nugget 22

The blessings of God knows no age limit

In 2 Chronicles 26:5 we see that Uzziah was sixteen years old when he became king and reigned for fifty-two years; some of which was during the life of the prophet Zechariah. As long as Uzziah sought the Lord, God caused him prosper.

Nugget 23

The blessings of God can be sought for regarding what has been spoken into one's life in the past; God can right all wrongs.

This is the prayer of Jabez.

> "Now Jabez was more honourable than his brothers, and his mother called his name Jabez, saying, "Because I bore him in pain." 10And Jabez called on the God of Israel saying, "Oh, that You would bless me indeed, and enlarge my territory, that Your hand would be with me, and that You would keep me from evil, that I may not cause pain!" So God granted him what he requested."

Nugget 24

The blessings of God must be sought from God, not man

Ezra 8:22

> *"The hand of God is upon all those for good who seek him … he answers their prayers."*

Nugget 25

You can remind God of His promises and put Him to the test

Malachi 3:10

AND

Nehemiah 1:11

> *"Lord, let your ear be attentive to the prayer of this your servant and to the prayer of your servants who delight in revering your name. Give your servant success today by granting him favour in the presence of this man."*

Nugget 26

You can ask God for blessings through divine favour

Divine favour can be obtained through sincere fasting and complete faith in God. For example, after her preparation period, Esther obtained favour in the sight of all who saw her (Esther 2:5).

Again, we see that, through divine favour, King Jehoiachin was released from prison (2 Kings 25:28-30):

> *"In the thirty-seventh year of the exile of Jehoiachin king of Judah, in the year Awel-Marduk became king of Babylon, he released Jehoiachin king of Judah from prison. He did this on the twenty-seventh day of the twelfth month. He spoke kindly to him and gave him a seat of honour higher than those of the other kings who were with him in Babylon. So Jehoiachin put aside his prison clothes and for the rest of his life ate regularly at the king's table. Day by day the king gave Jehoiachin a regular allowance as long as he lived."*

Nugget 27

God gives the ability of wealth creation through your spouse

"He who finds a wife finds a good thing and obtains favour from the Lord" (Proverbs 18:22).

The extent of a man's success can be measured by the genuine care for the wife. When a man finds a good woman, there can be an increase of favour in his life (Proverbs 31:11).

Nugget 28

You can walk into God's prosperity through your ministry

As we see in Leviticus 26:3-13, if we walk in God's shadow and keep His commandments, we will have:

- Rain in its season
- Land shall yield its produce
- The trees of the field shall yield their fruit etc.

Nugget 29

Tithing is a sure method of blessing

In light of Deuteronomy 14:22-23, the rewards of tithing are laid out in Malachi 3:10:

- Open the windows of heaven
- Pour out blessing
- Not enough room to take or receive it

You cannot out-give God. However, a man, who robs God, robs himself. Robbers usually go through an open window, and so God will shut His windows.

Nugget 30

Diligence and hard work are required for blessings

Diligence – The ant (Proverbs 6:6-8)

> *"Go to the ant, you sluggard; consider its ways and be wise! It has no commander, no overseer or ruler, yet it stores its provisions in summer and gathers its food at harvest."*

Proverbs 13:4

> *"The soul of the lazy man desires, and has nothing but the soul of the diligent shall be made rich."*

Proverbs 22:29

> *"Do you see a man who excels in his work? He will stand before Kings; he will not stand before unknown men."*

Nugget 31

You can find blessings at His feet

Song of Solomon 2:4

> *"He brought me to the banqueting house, and his banner over me was love."*

Nugget 32

You can find blessings by standing on the power in His word

Isaiah 55:10-11

> *"My word shall not return to me void."*

Isaiah 60:5-6

> *"The wealth of the Gentles shall come to you."*

Jeremiah 17:7-8

> *"Blessed is the man who trusts in the Lord."*

Jeremiah 29:11-12

> *"I know the thoughts that I think toward you, says the Lord, thoughts of peace and not of evil, to give you a future and hope."*

Nugget 33

You can find blessings by sowing into a sent prophet

Matthew 10:41 - Receive a prophet's blessing by receiving a prophet in the name of God.

Nugget 34

You can find blessings by knowing who God is and trusting in him at all times

Daniel 11:32b

"The people who know their God shall be strong, and carry out great exploits."

Nugget 35

You can find blessings through a healing process from backsliding

Hosea 14:4-6

"I will heal their backsliding, I will love them freely – He shall grow like the lily and lengthen his roots like Lebanon. His branches shall spread his beauty like olive tree, his fragrance like Lebanon."

Nugget 36-38

You can find blessings by standing

Prophetic blessings 1

Joel 2:25-26

> *"I shall eat in plenty and be satisfied."*

Prophetic blessings 2

Amos 9:13

> *"My ploughman shall overtake my reaper."*

Prophetic blessings 3

Obadiah 1:17

> *"On Mountain Zion there shall be deliverance, and there shall be holiness. The house of Jacob shall possess their possession."*

Nugget 39

You can find blessings by crying out to God

Jonah 2:2

> *"I cried out to the Lord because of my affliction, and he answered me out of the belly of Sheol, I cried out, and you heard my voice."*

Psalm 34:6

> "This poor man cried out, and the LORD heard him, And saved him out of all his troubles."

Nugget 40

"You can find blessings by doing what is good."

Micah 6:8

> "What is good, and what he requires of us: to do justly, to have mercy and to walk humbly with your God."

Nugget 41

God's vision for you brings wealth, wait for its time.

Habakkuk 2:3

> "But the vision is yet for an appointed time; but at the end it will speak, and it will not lie. Though it tarries, wait for it, because it will surely come, it will not tarry."

Nugget 42

You can activate God's blessing through your soul blessing Him

Psalm 103:1-5 (Bless the Lord o my Soul),

> *"Praise the Lord, my soul; all my inmost being, praise his holy name. Praise the Lord, my soul, and forget not all his benefits. Who forgives all your sins and heals all your diseases. Who redeems your life from the pit, and crowns you with love and compassion. Who satisfies your desires with good things, so that your youth is renewed like the eagles."*

Nugget 43

You can activate God's blessing through understanding and by laying claim to his word

Zephaniah 3:16-20

> *"On that day they will say to Jerusalem, 'do not fear, Zion; do not let your hands hang limp. The Lord your God is with you, the Mighty Warrior who saves. He will take great delight in you; in his love he will no longer rebuke you, but will rejoice over you with singing.' I will remove from you all who mourn over the loss of your appointed festivals, which is a burden and reproach for you. At that time I will deal with all who oppressed you. I will rescue the lame; I will gather the exiles. I will give them praise and honour*

in every land where they have suffered shame. At that time I will gather you; at that time I will bring you home. I will give you honour and praise among all the peoples of the earth when I restore your fortunes before your very eyes,' says the Lord."

Nugget 44

You can activate God's blessing by understanding the riches that you have in Christ Jesus

He has blessed us with every spiritual blessing in heavenly places (Ephesians 1:3).

Nugget 45

You can activate God's blessing by understanding the extent of his wealth

Haggai 2:8-9

"The silver is mine, the Gold is mine. The glory of this latter temple shall be greater than the former."

Nugget 46

You can pray a Prophetic Prayer and Confession to yourself, standing on the following scriptures:

Job 5:19-22

> "From six calamities he will rescue you; in seven no harm will touch you. In famine he will deliver you from death, and in battle from the stroke of the sword. You will be protected from the lash of the tongue, and need not fear when destruction comes. You will laugh at destruction and famine, and need not fear the wild animals."

Job 8:7

> "Though your beginning was small, yet your latter end would increase abundantly."

Job 8:20-22

> "He will fill your mouth with laughter and your lips with rejoicing."

Psalm 23:1

> "The Lord is my shepherd; I shall not want."

Psalm 34:10

> "But those who seek the Lord shall not lack any good thing."

Psalm 132:13-16

"The Lord has chosen Zion."

Psalm 37:25

"I have been young now I am old, I have never seen the righteous forsaken or his children beg for bread."

Lamentations 3:22-24

"Because of the Lord's great love we are not consumed, for his compassions never fail. They are new every morning; great is your faithfulness. I say to myself, "The Lord is my portion; therefore I will wait for him."

Ezekiel 36:29-30

"I will multiply the fruit of your trees."

2 Peter 1:3

"His divine power has given us everything we need for a godly life through our knowledge of him who called us by his own glory and goodness."

Nugget 47

You can activate God's blessing using the God kind of faith.

Mark 11:23-24 – God kind of faith;

> "So Jesus answered and said to them, "Have faith in God. For assuredly, I say to you, whoever says to this mountain, 'Be removed and be cast into the sea,' and does not doubt in his heart, but believes that those things he says will be done, he will have whatever he says. Therefore I say to you, whatever things you ask when you pray, believe that you receive them, and you will have them."

Hebrew 11:1

> "Faith is the substance of things hoped for, the evidence of things not seen.

Nugget 48

You can activate blessing not just wealth but the blessings of abundant life

John 10:10 – Give life, abundant life.

> "The thief does not come except to steal, and to kill, and to destroy. I have come that they may have life, and that they may have it more abundantly."

Nugget 49

Even when it does not seem like, understand and believe that it will work out for good

Romans 8:28

> *"All things work together for good to those who love God and are called according to his purpose."*

Nugget 50

You can activate blessing by understanding the seasons of life and the season for sowing.

Ecclesiastes 3:1

> *"To everything there is a season, a time for every purpose under heaven."*

Nugget 51

You can activate blessing by having a Godly focus

1 Corinthians 9:24

> *"Do you not know that those who run in a race all run, but one receives the prize? Run in such a way that you may obtain it."*

Nugget 52

You create the leverage for your blessings

2 Corinthian 9:6-11

"He who sows sparingly, will also reap sparingly."

Nugget 53

Understand and acknowledge God as the giver

James 1:17

"Every good gift and every perfect gift is from above, and comes from the Father of lights, with whom there is no variation or shadow of turning."

Nugget 54

Watch over the blessings and gifts that God has given you

Don't take them for granted and God will give more

2 Chronicles 25:6

"But if you go, be gone! Be strong in battle! Even so, God shall make you fall before the enemy; for God has power to help and to overthrow."

Ecclesiastes 9:10

"Whatever your hand finds to do, do it with your might."

Nugget 55

You can be blessed by walking in Wisdom

Colossians 4:5

"Walk in wisdom toward those who are outside, redeeming the time."

Proverbs 24:3

"A house is built by wisdom and becomes strong through good sense."

Nugget 56

You can be blessed by simply abounding in good works

2 Corinthians 9:8-11

"And God is able to make all grace abound toward you, that you, always having all sufficiency in all things, may have abundance for every good work."

Nugget 57

You can be continuously blessed remembering God

Deuteronomy 8:18

> "But remember the LORD your God, for it is he who gives you the ability to produce wealth, and so confirms his covenant, which he swore to your forefathers, as it is today."

Nugget 58

Wealth is not limited to money

Money is a spirit that must be tamed for it to produce godly wealth, or else it produces sin.

Luke 16:13

> "No servant can serve two masters. Either he will hate the one and love the other, or he will be devoted to the one and despise the other. You cannot serve both God and Money."

Nugget 59

God will not trust you with abundance if you have not been faithful in a little

See Luke 16:11

> "So if you have not been trustworthy in handling worldly wealth, who will trust you with true riches?"

Nugget 60

You can activate blessings by giving to the poor

See Matthew 19:21

> "If you want to be perfect, go sell what you have and give it to the poor, and you will have treasure in heaven; and come follow me."

Also Luke 11:41

Nugget 61

The prospering of our souls is the key to God more than anything else

Mark 8:36

> "What will it profit a man to gain all and lose his soul."

You can become God's silver and God's Gold

Malachi 3:3

> "He will sit as a refiner and a purifier of silver; He will purify the sons of Levi, and purge them as gold and silver, that they may offer to the Lord an offering in righteousness."

Nugget 62

God wants us to seek Him first

Matthew 6:33

God wants for us to seek first the kingdom of heaven and then this then activates "all other blessings."

Nugget 63

By trusting Him and by letting down your net, you can activate God's blessing

Luke 5:5-6

> "But Simon answered and said to Him, 'Master, we have toiled all night and caught nothing; nevertheless at Your word I will let down the net. And when they had done this, they caught a great number of fish, and their net was breaking."

TOTAL TRUST IN GOD can activate the blessings of prosperity.

Psalm 18:32-33

> "God is my strength and power, and he makes my way perfect, He makes my feet like the feet of deer and set me on my high places."

Also see 2 Corinthians 12:9, Exodus 15:2, Psalm 46:1 and Ephesians 6:10

Nugget 64

You can activate God's blessing through contentment

1 Timothy 6:6

> "Now godliness with contentment is great gain."

Luke 12:15

> "And He said to them, 'Take heed and beware of covetousness, for one's life does not consist in the abundance of the things he possesses.'"

Philippians 4:11

> 2Not that I speak in regard to need, for I have learned in whatever state I am, to be content."

Nugget 65

You can activate God's blessing through your first fruit

Deuteronomy 26:10

> *"And now I bring the firstfruits of the soil that you, O LORD, have given me."*

Place the basket before the LORD your God and bow down before him.

Nugget 66

You can activate God's blessing through divine purification

See Daniel 1:15

> *"And the end of the ten days their features appeared better and fatter in flesh than all the young men who ate the portion of the king's delicacies."*

YOUR PERSONAL ACTION SHEET

What are three key things you have learnt from reading this book?

I have learnt the follow:

1.

2.

3.

We learnt about the three categories of workers in Chapter 1: Common Workers, Managers; and Leaders. Which category of worker do you come under and why?

I come under this .... Category; this is the reason why,

....
....
....
....
....
....

BLOCKS

What do you need to do differently from each of the building blocks to help you move towards Financial Triumph (not more than 3)?

Spiritual building;

Character building;

Capacity building;

Life learning building blocks.

Do you have a mentor or a discipler and would you like to know more about mentoring and discipleship?

You can gain more information about the above, workshops and seminars tailored towards this book on www.tayoarowojolu.com